Economics of Money and Banking

Economics of Money and Banking

Arvind Sahani

CYBER TECH PUBLICATIONS
4264/3, Ansari Road, Daryaganj, New Delhi-110002 (India)
Ph.: 011-23244078. Fax: 011-23280028
E-Mail: cyberpublicationsdelhi@yahoo.com

ECONOMICS OF MONEY AND BANKING

Arvind Sahani

First Edition 2009

Published by :

G.S. Rawat for **Cyber Tech Publications**
4264/3, Ansari Road, Daryaganj, New Delhi-110002 (India)
Ph.: 011-23244078. Fax: 011-23280028
E-Mail: cyberpublicationsdelhi@yahoo.com

Printed at : Asian Offset Printers

Preface

It is impossible to appreciate how the financial system works without understanding risk. In the modern financial world, virtually all transactions transfer some degree of risk between two or more parties. These risk trades can be extremely beneficial, as they are in the case of insurance markets. But there is still potential for disaster. In 1998, risk-trading activity at Long-Term Capital Management (LTCM) threatened the stability of the international financial system.

Even though risk is absolutely central to an understanding of the financial system, most money and banking books give very little space to the topic. In contrast, this book devotes an entire chapter to defining and measuring risk.

Financial instruments are introduced early in the book, where they are defined based on their economic function. This approach leads naturally to a discussion of the uses of various instruments and the determinants of their value. Bonds, stocks, and derivatives all fit neatly into this framework, so they are all discussed together.

This approach solves one of the problems with existing texts, use of the term financial market to refer to bonds, interest rates, and foreign exchange. In its conventional microeconomic sense, the term market signifies a place where trade occurs, not the instruments that are traded. This book follows standard usage of the term market to mean a place for trade. It uses the term financial instruments to describe virtually all financial arrangements, including loans, bonds, stocks, futures, options, and insurance contracts. Doing so clears up the confusion that can arise when students arrive in a money and banking class fresh from a course in the principles of economics.

—Author

CONTENTS

1

The Nature and History of Money

MONEY: INTRODUCTION

What is economics about? If you ask someone who has not had an economics course, the person would probably answer "it's about money." And that's a very natural answer, since we have a monetary economy. The most obvious dimensions of economic activity are dimensions of money. Yet, in the first five chapters of this text, we have tried quite hard to avoid talking about money or monetary dimensions, saying that money is a veil, and that's true too--for many purposes, money is a veil.

But it is also important for economics to understand money and the monetary system, if only to be better able to look under the veil.

The importance of money reflects the most fundamental nature of a modern economic system. In a society without extended division of labor, in which every family produces almost all that they consume, there would be little need for money. However, in a society of the kind that Adam Smith envisioned--that is, a society like the one in which we live, with a very extended division of labor--it is hard to imagine living without a monetary system. This chapter explores some of what we economists think we know about money.

Trade and exchange are almost as old as the human species. We have, for example, archaeological evidence that flint blades and arrowheads were traded from modern Switzerland, where a distinctive form of flint is found, as far as eastern Siberia and southern Africa. But this trade was almost certainly by barter, that is, the direct exchange of one kind of good for another. In North America before 1700, widespread trade was carried on by a native American nation that was to give its name to the Canadian capital. In their own language, "Ottawa" means "he buys." And the Ottawa people bought, and sold, over a large part of North America, but, again, by barter.

It is difficult to imagine the trade of a modern society being carried on by barter. As Adam Smith wrote,

> *"Observe the accommodation of the most common artificer or day-labourer in a civilised and thriving country, and you will perceive that the number of people of whose industry a part, though but a small part, has been employed in procuring him this accommodation, exceeds all computation.... without the assistance and co-operation of many thousands, the very meanest person in a civilised country could not be provided,..." As a consequence, "In order to avoid the inconveniency of such situations, every prudent man in every period of society, after the first establishment of the division of labour, must naturally have endeavoured to... have at all times by him, besides the peculiar produce of his own industry, a certain quantity of some one commodity or other, such as he imagined few people would be likely to refuse in exchange for the produce of their industry."*

That commodity is money. Money enables us to exchange our own specialized products or services much more easily for the products and services of the thousands or millions of others we rely on for the goods and services we consume. Without a system of monetary exchange, it is hard to imagine that modern production, with extensive division of labor and collaboration and high labor productivity, could exist at all. Accordingly, in this chapter we explore modern monetary systems. We will first spend a bit of time on the history of money, and the evolution of modern monetary systems, and then on the workings of the modern systems. As always, we will focus mostly on the American system, but many of the principles will be applicable in other countries, and we shall try to indicate the ways in which the American system is unique.

Money is whatever serves as the "medium of exchange." That is, as the quotation from Adam Smith says, money is a commodity or token that everyone will accept in exchange for the things they have to sell. Different societies may have different monies. Some historical examples are:

- gold coins (in medieval Europe)
- cowrie shells (in West Africa)

The cowrie shells used in West Africa are small seashells. This may sound "quaint," but cowrie-money was very successful. It continued to be used into the twentieth century, after the West African countries had become colonies. The colonies were required to use European money, and they did--but when the European monetary systems collapsed in hyperinflation, the West African people went back to using their cowrie-money to get past the crisis. It was the cowrie-money that proved most reliable for many years of the twentieth century. We should say that the "commodity" that serves as money can be a purely symbolic token, like dollar bills in America. Indeed, all money has primarily symbolic value. Even the gold coins used in medieval Europe were probably valued more for their symbolic value than for the gold they contained. Symbolic or not, money is an asset. Thus we define:

Money

In any society, money is the asset, commodity or token, that serves as a medium of exchange.

As we have hinted, different societies have quite different money systems. The major historical types of money are

Commodity Moneys

These are moneys that have value in non-monetary uses equivalent to the monetary value of the commodity. Any commodity used as a medium of exchange is commodity money. Well-known examples are gold, copper and silver metals, but sea-shells (that is, cowrie shells) tobacco, and cigarettes have all been used. Historically, copper, gold and silver coins have been the most used in European and East Asian societies.

Metallic Coin

An example could be gold and silver coins that have values roughly equal to the price the metal would command as jewelry.

Other Commodities

As we have seen, seashells have been used as money, as have tobacco and, perhaps, oxen.

Fiat Money

Fiat money is a monetary standard (usually paper money) that people are required by law to accept as a medium of exchange and/or a standard of deferred payment. It is money by the "fiat"--the command--of the sovereign.

Fiduciary Money

Whenever a bank issues credible promises to pay in some other form of money, and the promises are transferable, they can circulate as money. Bank money is also called "fiduciary money," since it is based on the trust people have that the bank will keep faith (fides) and pay as promised. Fiduciary money may be based on promises to pay in commodity money (gold coin, for example) or in fiat money. We will go into much more detail later, because modern monetary systems are largely fiduciary. Two major instances of fiduciary money are

Bank Notes

These are bills issued by banks. They were widely used in the nineteenth century and are still used in some countries.

Checking Accounts

In our society, checks are acceptable as money, so by the definition of money--a commodity or token that serves as a medium of exchange--checks are money, just as real as any other kind of money.

Both fiat money and fiduciary money are tokens, of course, as distinct from commodity moneys. These token moneys are much the most important kinds of money in the modern world.

What about credit cards? In the United States at the close of the twentieth century, payments are often made by credit cards. But economists do not regard credit cards as money, because a credit card is not an asset.

What is a credit card? First, we need to answer another question: what is a "line of credit?" A "line of credit" is an agreement between a lender and a potential borrower, whereby the borrower can borrow up to some limit without any further approval. For example, if you were to build a house and act as your own prime contractor, you would need money to buy lumber and other supplies and to pay subcontractors from week to week. To do those things more conveniently, you might arrange with your banker to write checks for these expenses, even though you have no funds in the bank. Each check would be a loan, and the bank would honor them up to some agreed-on limit. Once your house is complete, you could refinance your loan as a long-term mortgage. This way, you wouldn't have to borrow the money (and thus pay interest on it) until you actually needed it. If you have a credit card with XYZ bank, that means you have a line of credit with that bank, and the card is the proof that the bank is willing to loan you money.

Of course, many people use credit cards for routine payments, and pay their bills within the "grace period," never paying interest. This has proved so convenient that "plastic money" is now a very common way of paying for transactions. But the banks don't find that very profitable, so they have been trying to move away from it. More and more people use "debit cards" instead. When you pay by "debit card," there is no loan, and the amount is taken directly from your checking account. Of course, the checking account is money. Debit cards work pretty much like credit cards--as long as you have money in your account!

But for an economist, the distinction between a credit card and a debit card is crucial. A debit card tansaction draws on assets that were there all along. By contrast, a credit card transaction creates a liability--not an asset--for the buyer, and the liability only comes into existence when the transaction takes place. It does not draw on pre-existing assets. And where there are no assets, there is no money.

We say traditionally that money has four major functions. It is a

Medium of Exchange

Whatever people usually give in exchange for the things that they buy is the medium of exchange. As we have seen, this is the function that defines money.

Unit of Account

The unit of account is the unit in which values are stated, recorded and settled. The differences between this and the medium of exchange may seem subtle, but there are a few cases in which the unit of account is different from the unit in which the medium of exchange is expressed. In Britain a few decades ago, Guineas were often used as the unit of account, while the medium of exchange was expressed in Pounds. Both Guineas and Pounds in turn could be expressed in shillings--the Pound was 20 shillings and the Guinea was 21 shillings. (British currency has since been redefined).

Standard of Deferred Payment

This is the unit in which debt contracts are stated. Deferred payment means a payment made in the future, not now. Here, again, it is usually the same as the medium of exchange, but not always. During periods of inflation, people may accept paper money for immediate payment, but insist on some other medium, such as real goods and services or gold, for deferred payment--because the medium of exchange would lose much of its value in the meanwhile.

Store of Value

Again, this is something that people keep in order to maintain the value of their wealth. Again, while it would usually be the same as the medium of exchange, in inflationary times other media might be substituted, such as jewelry, land or collectable goods. In this sense, money is "set aside" for the future.

A GRAPHIC TIMELINE OF THE HISTORY OF MONEY

Money has been used for something like 3000 years. City-states in the ancient near east had extensive trade from city to city, and they used precious metals as a medium of exchange. When trades were settled a certain amount of metal could be used to settle the difference. There was a problem of quality control, however. There were problems of determining that the quantity and purity of the metal was as agreed.

The answer was quality control and certification. The early kings of Lydia standardized the hunks of metal and guaranteed their quality by stamping the king's picture on them. These were the first coins. This guarantee of quality by the Lydian kingdom--already a rich and powerful one--was very successful, and made the Kingdom of Lydia even richer, indeed proverbially rich. Croesus and Midas--of all kings the most proverbially wealthy ones--were among the kings of Lydia.

But what Lydia could do, other kingdoms could also do. By 1000 AD, metallic coin monetary systems had spread through much of the old world.

As in so many other things, the Chinese were the innovators for the next step. The Chinese invented printing, and not too much later, they also invented paper money. It was widespread in China by around 1000 AD, but the Chinese abandoned it after about 1500, in the general decline of Chinese society after the Mongol conquest.

Paper money was to evolve much more indirectly in Europe, though.

Economists have traditionally explained the evolution of modern monetary systems by telling an old story, more or less a fictionalized version of the history of European money. Let's tell our own version of the old story, the story of the Bank of Fred.

Fred is a goldsmith, the only goldsmith in a small medieval city. As a goldsmith, he has a strong vault, to keep his own gold supplies in. Indeed, he has the only strong vault in town, and he stores the gold owned by other citizens for a small fee. A business that stores money in its vaults for a fee is called a bank of deposit. Naturally, to keep the records clear, Fred gives his customers receipts for their deposits.

After a while, some of Fred's customers use receipts for the gold they have deposited to make payments and settle debts. One customer may hand over a receipt in payment for a wagon, for example; and the wagon-maker may go down to Fred's Deposit Bank and take out his gold. But the wagon-maker may instead leave the gold on deposit, and pass the receipt on to the cooper (that is, the barrel-maker) to pay for some barrels. In this way, the receipts begin to circulate as money.

Thus, the receipts have become bank notes. Each receipt says, "Fred the Goldsmith will pay to the bearer, on demand, one gold florin," and these receipts are acceptable as money in Fred's town because the people have faith that Fred can and will honor that promise--that is, the bank-notes are "fiduciary money." A bank that issues bank-notes that circulate as fiduciary money is known as a "Bank of Issue," and Fred's Goldsmith Shop has become a bank of issue.

Bank of Issue

Then Fred makes a discovery. Fred finds that only a small percent of his receipts or bank notes are cashed in for gold in any given period. That means Fred can issue more notes than he has gold in his vaults, since he can (almost) always meet the small daily demand for redemption out of gold in the vaults.

One day Ronald the Peasant comes in to ask for a loan. Ronald is doing pretty well, and wants to buy a second ox so he can use a two-ox team to cultivate a larger field. Fred doesn't have any gold to loan--so he writes out some bank-notes and gives them to Ronald the Peasant as a loan. The ox-seller accepts the bank-notes in payment for the ox, and at the end of the year, Ronald sells some of his crop for bank-notes, and uses those bank-notes to repay the loan with interest. Fred has created money out of nothing (but trust)! And creating money is a profitable business. His profit from this business comes from interest on loans of these new banknotes.

In general, a bank of issue creates fiduciary money, either in the form of bank-notes or some other form, and lends them at a profit. Since the money is created from nothing, the interest may be mostly profits. Mostly, because banks have costs. In a system of competitive banking, competition may limit bank profits. But the Bank of Fred, a monopoly bank of issue in a small medieval town, faces no limit from competition.

The Limit

But there is a fly in the ointment all the same.

If many customers want to redeem their bank notes at once, the bank will not be able to comply. This is a "run" on the bank. The Bank of Fred will then be unable to redeem its notes, faith in them will collapse, and the bank-notes will cease to be money. Both Fred and his depositors will suffer losses if that happens, and perhaps be ruined. Fred has to be careful to keep enough gold coins in reserve to avoid this danger.

These reserves set a limit to the amount of money that Fred can create. Suppose experience has taught Fred that he needs to keep one Florin in the vault for every three banknotes he has issued. That is, Fred has adopted a reserve ratio--a ratio of reserves to money issue--of 1/3.

This determines how much money Fred can issue. If Fred has 1,000 Florins in the vault, then he can issue 3,000 Florins of bank-notes.

If someone deposits another 100 Florins, Fred would then be able to issue 300 new bank-notes. Fred would give 100 to the new depositor as receipts for his deposits, but the other 200 Florins would be available for Fred to loan out and so increase his profits.

Thus, in a system of fiduciary money, the amount of money in circulation generally is a multiple of the bank's reserves. The multiple is the inverse of the reserve ratio. In some systems, the law sets a minimum reserve ratio, but in others the reserve ratio is a matter of the banker's best judgment.

Truth

So much for the story. How true is it? How does the real history compare? There are differences of detail.

Probably the first fiduciary money in Europe was issued by a king, the "Holy Roman Emperor" Frederick II, known as "Stupor Mundi"--"the amazement of the world"--because of his famous intelligence. He was also the ruler of Sicily and southern Italy, where he lived and was beloved and very much trusted. This Mediterranean kingdom was very tolerant and prosperous, as a center of trade between Christian and Muslim nations; but suffered a recession that was believed to be a result of a shortage of silver coin currency. Frederick issued leather strips with his promise to pay a certain amount of silver coin on them, and they circulated as money. This was possible because the people trusted that their king would keep his promises. It does not seem that Frederick operated a bank of issue, though.

Among the real early bankers were the Medici, who started out as medical doctors, and ended as monarchs, and the Fuggers, who owned a silver mine. The use of bank receipts as money probably began mostly in international and interregional trade, with bankers at either end who cooperated by mail, as "correspondent banks."

But in a broad sense, the story is meant to illustrate the stages by which fiduciary money may have emerged. In that it is probably pretty accurate. And, in any case, it gives an accurate portrayal of the workings of a (monopoly) bank of issue in a system of fiduciary money. The Bank of Fred is a good example of a bank of issue.

The Gold Standard

By the 1700's, fiduciary money circulated widely in Western Europe, along with metallic coins. One of the most important banks of issue was the Bank of England, originally a private business. In the Napoleonic Wars, however, Britain had to resort to desperate measures to carry on the war. The Bank of England was nationalized and a system of paper "fiat money" was adopted.

After the war, Britain wanted to reconstruct a monetary system more like the prewar one, but a lot had changed. The government brought in a consultant--gentleman-economist David Ricardo. Ricardo designed a new, somewhat more streamlined monetary system.

In the new monetary system, paper Pound notes were the main medium of exchange. The Bank of England would hold a certain amount of gold for very Pound note in circulation. However, individual Pound notes could not be redeemed for gold coin. Pound notes would be convertible to gold only in large amounts, mainly for international trade. The notes would not be convertible to coin, but to bullion.

This is the "classical" gold standard of the nineteenth century--strictly speaking, not a gold coin system but a paper money system with the paper (fiduciary) money exchangeable for gold bullion.

Now let's see what the American Republic had in the way of a monetary system.

The Federal Reserve System

In the nineteenth century, America didn't have much of a monetary system at all.

During the 19th century, as we have seen, Britain was "on the gold standard." America was not. America was never on any very consistent monetary standard at all. (A course in American economic history would be necessary to go into the details of the various banking "reforms" and changes the country tried out during the nineteenth century). Remarkably, we did fairly well despite this, but there were some problems, and early in the twentieth century the Congress attempted to remedy them.

In 1913, Congress established the Federal Reserve System (the "fed") to be the American central banking system--the "bankers' bank" and main control on the monetary system.

The Federal Reserve system consists of 12 Banks for 12 districts in different parts of the country. According to law, each is a cooperative of the "member" banks. But for most practical purposes, "the fed" is a government agency. Its chairman and board of governors are appointed by the president with the consent of the Congress, as with many other government appointments. Its excess profits go to the treasury.

The federal reserve banks are also bankers' banks. In our system, "member" banks have deposits in the Federal Reserve, and these deposits are part of the member bank's reserves. The bank's reserves include the deposits in the Federal Reserve as well as cash in the bank's vaults, and these reserves take the place of the gold coins the Bank of Fred held in its vaults to assure that it would be able to redeem its banknotes. By controlling the amount of reserves, and regulating the reserve ratio, the Federal Reserve System controls the American Money Supply.

On an earlier page, We saw that there are three basic kinds of money: commodity, fiat, and fiduciary money. Which kind is modern American money? The answer is that it is a mixture of fiat and fiduciary money. Bank reserves, federal reserve notes and deposits in the Federal Reserve system, are fiat money. Checking accounts are fiduciary money, based on the faith that the checks will be accepted. Since we have many banks, a key problem is to assure that a check written on one bank will be accepted as a deposit in another bank. The Federal Reserve system assures this by controlling the reserves and "clearing" checks and deposits among the different banks. (We will see in the next few pages how this happens). Since he can deposit my check in his own bank, and write checks to make his own payments, the merchant who sells me goods or services is willing to accept my check. Federal reserve notes are fiat money, and are acceptable to banks because they are legal reserves. Since it is acceptable to banks, the dollar bill is acceptable to people in general.

Something similar could be said about most developed economies. In the modern world, money is not a commodity but a service provided by banks.

Components of the American Money Supply

We have said that checking accounts are money in modern America. So is currency (federal reserve notes and coins), of course. What are the proportions of these different forms of money, and how large is the American money supply? In June, 1996, the proportions were as shown in Table 1, according to the Federal Reserve Bank of St. Louis.

Table 1

currency	379.3
checking accounts	729.3
of which:	
demand deposits	413.6
other checkable accounts (NOW accounts, etc)	315.7
travellers' checks	8.7
total	1117.3

"Demand deposits" and "other checkable accounts" are both checking accounts--the difference is in the history of the banks that issue them, and isn't very important any more. We also include travellers' checks, which are even more like currency than ordinary checks are; but they are a small component. The figures in this table are in billions, so we see that the total of currency, checking accounts, and travellers' checks is over one trillion at the mid-way point of the year 1996.

What all these checkable accounts and travellers' checks have in common is that they are obligations of banks to individuals or non-bank companies. The checking account is an obligation of the bank to honor the checks, as long as the account is enough. Even currency, is, in a sense, an obligation of the Federal Reserve Banking system--though in this case the obligation is toward the banks, in that the Federal Reserve System is obligated to accept currency as deposits toward the banks' reserves. But there are other bank obligations that are not included: savings accounts, for example. One might ask: should still other kinds of bank obligations be considered as money and included in the money supply? Some economists feel they should, and the result is that we have several different concepts of the money supply. The list we have given above, amounting to 1117.3 billion dollars in 1996, is called "M1" in the conventional system of measurement of the money supply. But many economists rely more on a broader concept of money known as M2, which includes savings deposits, small time deposits (a lot like savings deposits) and money market fund balances. Table 2 shows the makeup of M2 in June, 1996:

Table 2

M1	1117.3
savings deposits	1206.5
small time deposits	928.0
retail money fund balances	496.0
Total: M2	**3747.9**

There are other, still broader concepts of money, that include other kinds of bank obligations, but we shall not go into more detail here.

You may ask, what about credit cards, so-called "plastic money?" Savings accounts are included in M2 for two reasons: they are bank obligations, assetd of the person who has the account, and they are also good substitutes for checking accounts (or currency). Credit cards are also good substitutes for checking accounts and currency, but they are different in other ways.

As we have seen, a credit card is a "line of credit"--that is, an agreement with a bank whereby the bank prequalifies the card-holder for a loan, whenever the card-holder wants to take it out, at agreed-upon terms. But it does seem that the emergence of credit cards as an important means of payment has changed our money system in some important ways.

In the rest of this chapter, we will use the M1 concept of money--currency plus checkable deposits. We will ignore the small amount of travellers' checks.

A DECENTRALIZED BANKING SYSTEM

As we said, the "Bank of Fred" was a monopoly bank of issue. In the real modern world, however, we have many decentralized and competitive banks of issue. That makes the real world a little more complex than Fred's fictional world.

Table 3A:

First National Bank of Enumclaw		
1	Deposits	60000
	reserves	10000
2	new deposit	10000
	total deposits	70000
	required reserves	11666.6667
	actual reserves	20000
	excess	8333.33333

Let's see how an increase in monetary reserves leads to the creation of new money in a banking system like the modern American one. Suppose that the reserve ratio is 1/6. Then Joe Blow returns from Russia, where he has sold his used Hewlett Packard computer for $10,000 in crisp $100 bills. Joe takes the money down to his home-town bank, the First National Bank of Enumclaw, and deposits it. The bank in turn deposits the new $10,000 in its Federal Reserve Bank, increasing its reserves. Let's see what happens.

In Table 3, part A, step one is before Joe makes his deposit. Step two is after the deposit is made. The deposit increases the bank's deposits and reserves by the same amount, $10,000. But with a 1/6 reserve ratio, the bank only needs to keep $1,666.67 of reserves against Joe's deposit, and so it has excess reserves. And excess reserves are an opportunity. With excess reserves, the bank can increase its profits by making some loans.

Next Step: James Roe applies for a loan of $8,333.33 to buy a used Yugo.

CREATING MONEY

So the bank lends James $8,333.33 and gives him a checking account. This is created money! But they can do it, because their books balance. They have acquired an asset--James' promise to repay, with interest--and a liability--James' checking account--and the two just balance. Plus, they still have some excess reserves! But, as we will see in the next page, they can't loan any more without running into difficulties. The details for Step 3 are shown in Table 3 part B below.

Table 3B

First National Bank of Enumclaw		
3	loan	8333.33333
	total deposits	78333.3333
	required reserves	13055.5556
	actual reserves	20000
	excess	6944.44444

James Spends his Checking Account

Of course, James hasn't borrowed money for his health. Let's see what happens when James spends the loan. He writes a check to Enumclaw Clean Cars, and the car salesman deposits the check in his own bank, the Second National Bank of Enumclaw.

The Second National bank will send this check as a deposit in the Federal Reserve Bank for the district, thus increasing their own reserves. As we see in Table 3 part C below, this leaves the Second National Bank with excess reserves.

Table 3C

Second National Bank of Enumclaw		
4	Deposits	60000
	reserves	10000
5	new deposit	8333.33
	total deposits	68333.33
	required reserves	11388.8883
	actual reserves	18333.33
	excess	6944.44167

Back at First National...

Remember, First National had some excess reserves when we left them. Why didn't they increase their profits by lending still more money?

To get its money, Second National will deposit James' check with the Federal Reserve, and the Fed will deduct that amount from First National's account, reducing First National's reserves. This is called "clearing" the check.

Let's see what happens when Second National presents James' check for clearing:

Table 3D

First National Bank of Enumclaw		
	deposits	78333.3333
6	check clears	-8333.3333
	total deposits	70000
	required reserves	11666.6667
	actual reserves	11666.6667
	excess	0

As we see in Table 3 part D, after the check is cleared, First National is left with exactly its required reserves--no excess.

That's why First National limited its lending at the first stage--the bank management knew that the loan check would clear, and they had to allow for that in lending from their excess reserves.

They are left with a profitable $8,333.33 loan as an asset, and the money supply (checking accounts) has increased by $10,000 (the initial deposit) plus $8,333.33 (James Roe's loan) = $18,333.33.

But Second National Bank has excess reserves, and they can increase their profits by making a loan.

THE MONEY MULTIPLIER

But the money creation isn't over. Remember, we left Second National Bank with some excess reserves. So they can make a new loan and increase their profits--and the cycle starts over. And the cycle continues, indefinitely, with smaller and smaller amounts of new money creation at each stage, as shown in Table 4.

We see that the upper limit of total new money is six times the original influx of reserves. This is the money multiplier. It is the inverse of the reserve ratio.

Table 4

		Running Total
Joe's Deposit	$10,000.00	$10,000.00
First National	$8,333.33	$18,333.33
Second National	$6,944.44	$25,277.78
Third National	$5,787.04	$31,064.81
Fourth National	$4,822.53	$35,887.35
Fifth National	$4,018.78	$39,906.12
Sixth National	$3,348.98	$43,255.10
...	...	...
Thirty-Fifth National	$16.93	$59,915.35
finally...		$60,000.00

BANKS

This example is a bit simplified, like the story of "the Bank of Fred," but like that story it illustrates the working of a fiduciary money system--in this case the modern American one. Details, such as the required reserve ratio and the specific assets that can be counted as reserves, may change from time to time.

But the principles of the system are those illustrated in the example. The key points are

- Checking accounts are money, fiduciary money created by banks
- Creation of fiduciary money is limited by the supply of bank reserves
- Bank reserves are obligations of the Federal Reserve, including deposits and vault cash
- Checks are "cleared" by the Federal Reserve by transferring deposits from the bank that issued the check to the bank that deposits it

- A bank that has excess reserves may be able to create money and loan it, by establishing a checking account in the amount of the loan
- Nevertheless, banks have to limit their lending to allow for "clearing" through the Federal Reserve.
- An increase in reserves, for example by importing currency from abroad, increases the total money supply by a multiple of the increase in reserves
- The multiple is the inverse of the required reserve ratio.

The Federal Reserve system thus can control the total supply of money by controlling the supply of bank reserves. Let's see how this is done.

OPEN MARKET COMMITTEE

The money supply is controlled by the Open Market Committee of the Federal reserve system, the FOMC. This body is called the "open market committee" because it buys and sells government bonds on the open market. This open market activity influences the supply of bank reserves and thus the money supply.

Suppose that the board of governors of the Federal Reserve System has decided to increase the money supply. Here is how the FOMC would carry out that policy:

1. The FOMC buys bonds.
2. It pays for the bonds with a check on the Fed.
3. The check is an addition to bank reserves.
4. With more reserves, banks create more money.

For example, suppose the FOMC buys a $1000 bond from Jane Roe, and gives Jane a check on the Federal Reserve Bank of New York in return for the bond. Jane makes a deposit in her bank, First National of Enumclaw. First National will then deposit the check in the Fed (actually in the Federal Reserve Bank of San Francisco, which serves

Enumclaw) and thus First National's reserves are increased. This increase in reserves leads to more loans and a multiple increase in the supply of money, in the same way as the example we just looked at.

CUTTING THE MONEY SUPPLY

Now suppose instead the decision is instead to reduce the money supply, perhaps as a means of avoiding inflation. Then the method is just the reverse.

1. The FOMC sells bonds.
2. The check written to pay for the bonds is cleared through the FED.
3. This reduces bank reserves.
4. With less reserves, banks must cut back on money creation.

In this case, Jane Roe buys a $1,000 bond from the holdings of the Federal Open Market Committee, and pays for it with a check on her account in the First National Bank of Enumclaw. This check goes directly to the Fed, which "clears" it by reducing the deposits in the name of the First National Bank of Enumclaw. First National of Enumclaw will in turn reduce Jane Doe's account by $1,000. Let's see what that does to First National's required reserves in the Table 4:

Table 4

First National Bank of Enumclaw		
1	Deposits	60000
	reserves	10000
2	check cleared	1000
	total deposits	59000
	required reserves	9833.33
	actual reserves	9000
	shortfall	833.33333

The problem is that the reduction of $1,000 in Jane Roe's deposit reduces the required reserves by only a fraction of $1,000, in this case by one-sixth. Thus, First National is left with $833.33 less reserves than it needs. How are they to get the reserves they require? In the short run, they can borrow reserves; but in the longer run, they will have to turn down some applications for loans.

For example: on the next day, two customers visit First National. Richard Bowe repays his loan of $833.33 (interest included) and Donald Lowe (who has good credit) applies for a loan of $833.33 to buy a new television set. If the bank had plenty of reserves, they would probably "recycle" the $833.33 repayment by making the loan to Donald--but they have to turn down Donald's loan application and apply the amount to their reserves instead.

Donald goes on and buys the TV set anyway, writing a check on his account at Second National. But that means Second National's reserves are reduced, and they, too, have to cut back on loans. And thus the decrease in reserves leads, again, to a multiple reduction in the money supply--eventually a $6,000 reduction, assuming, again, a 1/6 required reserve ratio.

MONETARY STANDARDS

But why all this concern? Granted that a monetary system is essential for a modern economy, why did nineteenth-century England go to such trouble to fine-tune the quantity of money in circulation? Why is it so important that the Fed limit money issue by American banks?

The answer comes in two stages.

- From many points of view, the effectiveness of the monetary system requires a fairly stable average price level. As we have seen in a previous chapter, inflation can and sometimes has destroyed the purchasing power of a monetary unit very rapidly.

- The danger of inflation was seen as being connected to the quantity of money in circulation by way of the "quantity theory of money."

Let's digress a bit and take a look at that theory.

THE QUANTITY THEORY OF MONEY

We have not said much in detail about the impact of changes in the monetary system on the market system. Modern ideas on that will have to wait for a later chapter on "Monetary Policy." But these modern ideas grow out of an idea from the Classical Economists, known as the Quantity Theory of Money.

The quantity theory is based on the identity

$$M*V = p*RGDP$$

where M is the quantity of money in circulation, p*RGDP is nominal GDP, and V is the "velocity of money." The idea here is that each transaction will require a certain amount of money to carry it out.

The amount of money for a given transaction will depend on the habits and customs of the time and place, but will be fairly stable in the short run.

In turn, the number of transactions (of each specific type) will be roughly proportionate to production, that is, to RGDP. So we have a predictable relationship between the production, RGDP, and the quantity of money needed to finance and sell it. An increase in the price level would proportionately increase the amount of money needed to do that.

The equation

$$M*V = p*RGDP$$

is an identity because V is defined as p*RGDP/M. But early quantity theorists held that V is a constant, which means that the demand for money is proportional to nominal income--an hypothesis which we can test against the facts.

Over the twentieth century as a whole, this hypothesis has done pretty well as a first approximation, though some monetary economists feel that the relationship has been less predictable, for the U. S. A, in the last decades of the twentieth century.

THE QUANTITY THEORY AND THE PRICE LEVEL

The classical economists believed that the supply of money would determine the price level. To see how that would work, we can rearrange the "quantity equation,"

M*V = p*RGDP

And get

p = M*V/RDGP

If the money supply is given, then, according to the rearranged quantity equation, the price level depends on production and the "velocity" constant. In turn, many classical economists treated RGDP as a constant, on the following reasoning:

- They assumed that the employment of labor would be determined by the supply and demand for labor, along with the wage in purchasing power terms.
- The employment of labor, together with the productivity of labor, would determine production as measured by RGDP.
- Since since the supply and demand and productivity of labor are al independent of the price level and the quantity and velocity of money, production would also be independent of those things, that is, a constant so far as the quantity equation is concerned.

This is illustrated with a diagram on the next page:

QUANTITY THEORY DIAGRAM

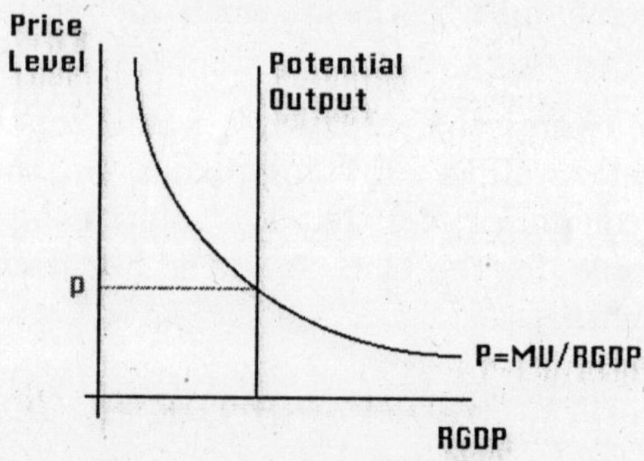

Figure 1: Money, the Price Level, and Output

In the figure, production (RDGP) is measured on the horizontal axis and the price level is on the vertical axis. Thus the relationship p=MV/RGDP is represented by a hyperbolic curve, shown in green. The vertical red line represents the production determined by the supply and demand and productivity of labor. Where the two intersect, the quantity equation is fulfilled, and that is understood as the equilibrium price level. Thus p, shown in yellow, is the price level corresponding to the quantity of money in the diagram.

CHANGING THE QUANTITY OF MONEY

The point of the theory is less to say what the price level is, with a given money supply, and more to predict the results of changes in the money supply. So what happens when the money supply increases?

The new money supply is shown in light green. We have an increase in the money supply, and the result is that the price level rises from p to p'.

This is a pretty simple, and oldfashioned, version of the Quantity Theory. Before we move on, let's update the quantity theory, and as we do so, we will learn a couple of important details about our monetary system.

An increase in the money supply is shown in Figure 2 below:

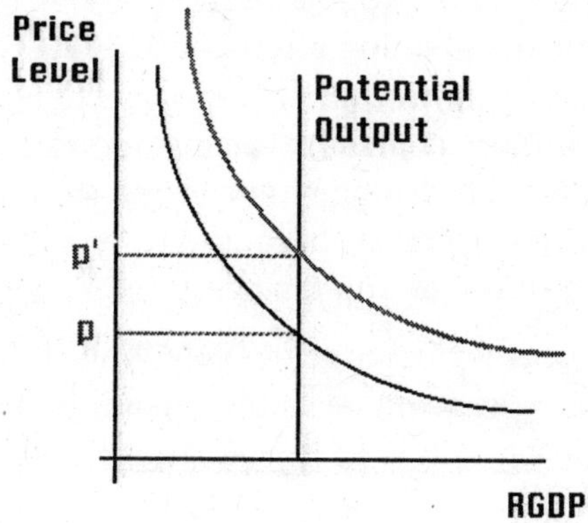

Figure 2: Increasing the Money Supply

A MORE MODERN VIEW

Let's think a little further about that "velocity." Will it really be a constant?

There is no magic in algebra--evil magic or good!--but sometimes tinkering with an equation changes the perspective. In place of

M*V = p*RGDP

let us write the equivalent

M = p*RGDP*(1/V)

On the left hand side, M is the quantity of money that people want to keep as an asset--the total of bills in their pockets, dollars in their checking accounts, and so on. In the terms used by modern quantity theorists of money, M is the "demand for money." Thus, on the right hand side, (1/V) is the demand for money per dollar of transaction. That is, (1/V) is the amount of money assets an average person needs to keep (in her purse, pocket or bank accounts) for every dollar of goods and services that she or he buys, during a year.

But why should a person want to hold any amount of money? The answer is convenience, of course--it is more convenient to keep a certain amount of money on hand than to find other means of doing business. Monetary economists say that money economizes on "shoe leather costs," and I guess they visualize a person having to walk back to the bank to get some more money out of his saving account in order to make a purchase, because he hasn't had enough money in his pocket or his checking account.

But "shoe leather costs" can be balanced against other kinds of costs. Checking accounts usually don't earn as much interest as other (less convenient) kinds of bank accounts, and bills in your pocket or your mattress don't earn any interest at all. Thus, the interest you don't earn is an "opportunity cost" of holding money. If interest rates go up, then the opportunity cost of holding money also goes up, and we would think that 1/V and the demand for money would drop. So V (or 1/V) isn't always a constant after all.

INTEREST AND THE DEMAND FOR MONEY

Another word for the convenience of money is "liquidity." The more convenient, safe and flexible an asset is, as a means of payment, the more "liquid" we say it is. Money is the most "liquid" of assets.

So the "demand for money" is a balancing act. If a person keeps more of her assets in a convenient account, she will gain liquidity--save on "shoe leather" costs--but she will sacrifice the higher interest she could get on a less convenient account.

What will happen then if the interest rate on the less convenient accounts drops? Liquidity is less costly--the opportunity cost of the more convenient accounts is lower--and when liquidity is less costly we suppose that a person will demand more liquidity. Thus the demand for money would rise (velocity would drop) when the interest rate on non-liquid assets drops.

John Maynard Keynes expressed this idea with the "liquidity preference curve," and modern central banks, like the American Fed, base their operations on the idea that the demand for liquidity rises when the interest rate (on non-liquid assets like bonds) drops.

THE LIQUIDITY PREFERENCE CURVE

Here is a diagram to illustrate the "liquidity preference" idea.

In the diagram, we show the quantity of money on the horizontal axis and the interest rate on the vertical axis. For example, if the rate of interest is Ra, people want to hold Ma of money, whereas if the rate of interest were to go down to Rb, people would increase their demand for monetary assets to Mb.

The Fed can use this relationship, in reverse, to influence the interest rate. Suppose the Fed sets the total quantity of money at Ma. Then people will try to shift their assets out of the less liquid accounts into liquid money accounts as long as the rate of interest is less than Ra, or in reverse, to buy nonliquid assets whenever the rate of interest is greater than Ra. Since they cannot all shift their assets at once--the total quantity of assets of each kind is known--their competition for liquid or nonliquid assets will drive the interest rate to Ra. We may say that Ra is the "equilibrium interest rate" with a money supply of Ma. If the Fed wants to push interest rates down to Rb, they would increase the money supply to Mb.

There are two points of controversy about this.

- There may be a lower limit to how far the Fed can push the interest rates down. In the diagram, the demand for money increases without any limit as the interest rate falls toward Rt. Thus, no matter how much the Fed increases the money supply, it could never push the interest rate below Rt. Rt is called "liquidity trap." Some economists have questioned the possibility of a "liquidity trap;" but others observe that the Japanese economic system, in the late 1990's, behaved very much like it was at the "liquidity trap" interest rate level. In any case, interest rates can never go lower than zero, and Japanese interest rates in the late 1990's were sometimes so low that the zero lower limit would be relevant.

- The Fed can use the liquidity preference relationship to influence interest rates only to the extent that the relationship is stable, or at least predictable. But some economists believe that it is very unstable and unpredictable--a source of trouble rather than a means of control. In the fall of 1998, with the collapse of a major "hedge fund," and again just before January 1 2000, the Fed believed that there would be bid increases in liquidity preference. Indeed, for a short period in 1998, it seemed as if the U. S. economy had a liquidity trap at an interest rate of several percent. But because they predicted these changes, the Fed adjusted the money supply to keep the interest rates more nearly stable, and they were successful on the whole.

IS IT CORRECT?

How does the quantity theory match up with the facts? So far as the very largest increases in the price level are concerned--the so-called hyperinflations--it is at least a good first approximation. There have been no hyperinflations without enormous increases in the supply of money. The quantity theory explains that two ways. First, the large increase in the demand for money would increase the price level proportionately if V were constant. Second, V probably would not stay constant. Remember, 1/V is the amount of money people want to hold, per dollar of purchases, for convenience. But if that money is losing its value through inflation, the convenience of holding money comes at a higher and higher cost in terms of purchasing power. Thus, as people try not to hold money for very long, V increases without limit and 1/V goes to zero--making the upward pressure on prices all the worse.

And some economists take the view that all changes in the price level are best explained by changes in the money supply, saying that "Inflation is always and everywhere a monetary phenomenon." But this view remains controversial in economics, and some economists would argue that inflation can have other important causes, and that the quantity theory of money is oversimple.

But now let's take a closer look at the institutions that control the supply of money in a modern economy: banks and the Federal Reserve System, often known as the Fed.

WHAT ABOUT GOLD?

This is a complex system of institutions that has grown up over centuries in a mixture of blind evolution, design and deliberate reform. Its complexity and non-obvious nature cause anxiety to some of us who have to rely on it. Can such a make-shift really work? Wouldn't it be smarter to go back to simple, obvious gold coins? The answer is, probably not:

It is true, experience has taught us, that any monetary system with a large component of government fiat money is vulnerable to inflation. All of the great hyperinflations have been associated with huge increases in the amount of money in circulation, specifically because of government creation of fiat money. On the other hand, we have plenty of examples of well-managed and very stable modern monetary systems. The dollar ranks pretty high in this regard, but if the dollar isn't "hard" enough for you, the German Mark and the Swiss Franc in the second half of the twentieth century must have been about as stable as it is possible for a monetary system to be.

On the other hand, gold is not perfect as a monetary system either. Historically, new discoveries have propelled vast inflations. Governments have clipped and adulterated the coins, and (in more modern history) have adopted the gold standard only to drop it when it is no longer politically convenient.

If we have a government with enough self-discipline to stick to a rigorous gold standard, it will probably do equally well with a managed bank-money system. Finally, a real cost of a gold coin system is the resource cost of "digging it up in Nevada to bury it again in Fort Knox." While a managed bank money system has costs too, at least the costs of digging are avoided.

THE MODERN MONETARY SYSTEM: SUMMARY

If this chapter has given a basic understanding of the nature of a modern monetary system, then it has done its job. By way of review, here are some of the basic points.

- Modern money is a token, not a commodity with a value in non-monetary use. This is not to say that our money has no value. On the contrary: the value of money is what it will buy--and as modern money will buy a range of goods gold coins could not have bought, it is, in a sense, far more valuable.
- Modern money is a mixture of fiduciary money (obligations of banks) and fiat money issued by government or quasi-government organizations.
- Fiduciary money is a service produced by banks, so-called "banks of issue." These banks create money at some multiple of the reserves they have available to pay claims.
- Complex as this system is, it is hard to imagine an alternative system that would clearly be more stable, workable, and cheap to administer than a well-administered fiduciary money system.

- In our system, money creation is controlled and managed by the central banks, such as the Federal Reserve System. The Central Banks control the creation of money by regulating bank reserves and controlling the amount of reserves available.
- The quantity theory of money teaches us that it is important that the quantity of money be controlled and not increase too fast. Even if the quantity theory is not exactly true, there is no question that the great hyperinflations have been the consequences of uncontrolled increases in the quantity of token money.

In conclusion, the monetary system, complex or simple as it may be, is an essential part of any modern economic system. Without a functioning monetary system, modern production literally collapses. This key component of the market system deserves the time and study required to understand it thoroughly.

2

International Trade

This chapter addresses the interdependence of different nations through international trade, including the motives for trading rather than relying on domestic production and some implications for the relations among national monetary systems.

There are a lot of introductory economics texts. Why write another? One reason is as obvious as your computer screen: this will be an experiment in the use of a new technology, the World-Wide Web, to present the basic text materials. There are things we can do with this technology that we cannot do with print. But there is a danger in this. As a teacher of economics, I don't want my students to focus on the technology and miss the economics! And I have sometimes seen that happen. But everything new has risks, and we will just have to be alert for this problem and do what we can to avoid it, you and I.

Another reason is to present the material in a different and, we hope, better way. Economics is a conversation that has been going on for over two hundred years. And the conversation is continuing today. There are issues that are not resolved, but there are also some very important things we have learned. The conversation is not limited to professional economists, of course, but involves responsible citizens in our democratic republics. The main objective of this text is to introduce the student to that conversation, as professional economists have participated in it, and thus enable the student to participate more effectively (as a citizen and manager) in the discussion as it goes on. In some fields, the introductory material is presented as a historical survey--the basic ideas presented as they came along in the history of the subject, and put in context that way.

Philosophy is an example of this. In other fields, the basic texts are written as if the field had no history at all. Mathematics is an example of this. Economics texts are usually somewhere in the middle, but a little closer to the mathematics end of the spectrum. In thirty years of teaching economics, I have come to the conclusion that we need to come a little closer to the philosophy end of the spectrum, and this text will try to put economics in the context of that ongoing conversation.

Another reason to approach economics this way is that economics is a field full of controversy. There is a joke that economists can never agree with one another. That's not quite fair--there is much that economists do agree on, and much of that is important--but there are also issues that remain open in economics, issues on which well-informed, intelligent people can disagree. And that should not be a surprise. These issues are even more controversial among the general public. I believe we can understand these issues in a more even-handed way by seeing economics clearly as a conversation--usually with two or more sides.

In most studies the first step is to answer the questions: what and how? That is, what is the subject matter to be studied? What is economics? And then: how is economics studied? What methods do economists use?

In both of those things, this text will be a bit old-fashioned. I will define economics very much as the classical economists of the eighteenth and nineteenth century defined it. Old-fashioned as this is, it is also right up to date with some of the best economic research of the 1990's.

As to the "how," the big question is the role of scientific method. Is economics a science? Certainly it has a scientific aspect, but we believe it has other aspects as well. The scientific aspect of economics has developed enormously during the twentieth century. All the same, there are other aspects that go beyond science, and we must deal with those aspects too. Thus, we will need an approach that can deal with the nonscientific aspects. In this, again, we find ourselves closer to the classical economists of previous century, though we are also up to date with current researchers who say that economics is a conversation in which all aspects, scientific and otherwise, can and must be discussed.

Of course, we do not want to turn the clock back. Economists have learned many very important things in the twentieth century. But--as we move toward the twenty-first--one objective of this text is to put this learning in the context of the longer and broader conversation.

This chapter will enlarge on the what and how. First: what is economics? Then: how do economists reason?

WHAT IS ECONOMICS?

What is Economics? We might take our definition from the father of modern economics, Adam Smith. He entitled his famous book An Inquiry Into the Nature and Causes of the Wealth of Nations. That is not a bad description of the subject matter of economics, but many modern economists have tried to find a more logical or scientific definition.

Smith was, in many ways, the founder of modern economics. He wrote at a time when the industrial revolution was just beginning to transform European society. He observed that, in his own society, economic development could bring about a widespread prosperity, and yet other countries, and even some districts of an advanced country such as Britain, could lag behind in poverty. It was never difficult to account for poverty--poverty had been the condition of most people since time immemorial--but what could account for this prosperity? This was the question Smith put to himself, and in his time it was the central question of economics.

This hyperbook will follow Smith's example. We will be inquiring into the nature and causes of the wealth of nations, and that inquiry will be our definition and our answer to the question, "what is economics?"

Yet economics is a field full of controversy, and even the definition of the field has been a subject of controversy. We will take a look at the controversy before the end of this chapter. For now, however, let us follow the line of thought in the definition. What does it mean to study the nature and causes of the wealth of nations?

"Universal Opulence"

In his great book, An Inquiry into the Nature and Causes of the Wealth of Nations, Adam Smith took this question as his first subject: what is it that causes production of goods and services to increase with time, so that nations become wealthy rather than poor? According to Smith, "It is the great multiplication of the productions of all the different arts,... which occasions, in a well-governed society, that universal opulence which extends itself to the lowest ranks of the people." (Wealth of Nations, Modern Library edition, p. 11) Smith's objective was to learn more about the "multiplication of productions." For him this was the point of economics.

When the production of goods and services for the market grows bigger, this is what we call "economic growth." If production grows fast enough, then we will have more production per person; and this is called a "rise in the standard of living." When Adam Smith talked about "the wealth of nations," modern economists would talk about a high and rising standard of living.

We will spend a few pages on this. What can lead to growing production?

CAUSES OF GROWING PRODUCTION

Here are some of the things which may help a nation to become more productive and thus "wealthier." The list may not cover the whole story (we don't know everything) and the different items on the list may overlap and certainly are interdependent. But the list will serve to organize our "inquiry. "

- increase in quantities of resources available
- discovery of new technologies
- increases in the division of labor and specialization
- improvements in the allocation of existing resources
- increases in the rate of use of existing resources

The last two causes will be the subjects of most of the chapters in this hyperbook; accordingly, we will leave them for later. The first three were also the ones which Adam Smith stressed, But not in the order of importance that Smith gave them. Smith put the division of labor first. In this chapter, we will follow the more modern approach, and put resources first.

Resources

Generally, the market economy can grow larger if any of the resources available to it becomes more plentiful. In other words, we can produce more outputs if we use more inputs. Traditionally, economists speak of three major kinds of resources, or, in other (and more traditional) words, three factors of production. The three "factors of production" are

- land
- labor
- and capital

Land

By convention, economists include in the category "land" both :

- the "original and indestructible powers of the soil" and
- natural resources, such as coal, oil, and metallic ores.

There are, of course, some important differences. Coal and oil, once they are dug out or the ground and burned, are gone for ever. In other words, they are "wasting resources." On the other hand, the fertility of the soil does not have to be a wasting resource, if the farmer uses farming methods which maintain fertility. But this difference is not absolute. Copper ores, for example, may be used and then recycled.

Labor

We may not think of labor as a resource, and of course it differs from the other two categories, since labor is directed human action and thus requires that the human being have some motivation. (Money is one possible motivation, of course, and a common one). Land does not require motivation. But, from several points of view, labor is the most important resource. From the point of view of cost, it is quite important. In the American economy, labor costs amount to something between two-thirds and three-quarters of costs (net of raw materials). Labor is also important to most of us because it is the resource from which we expect to get our living.

Capital

Capital consists of all goods produced by human labor (with other resources) and used in the production of still more goods and services; in other words, produced means of production. Some examples are

- machinery
- houses and other buildings
- grapevines, fruit trees and hogs on the hoof
- and human capital

RESOURCES AND THE WEALTH OF NATIONS

One way to increase production is to increase the quantity of resources available. Of these three resources, the supply of labor and capital can be increased. By contrast, the quantity of land and natural resources on the planet cannot be increased.

It is true that we can discover more natural resources--even if we cannot, like Columbus, discover a new supply of agricultural land on this planet. Discovery is not quite the same thing as creation, though; we can discover, but cannot create, more land and natural resources. We can create more capital and give birth to more labor.

An increase in the population increases the supply of labor, but, as the saying goes, every additional person is also an additional mouth to feed. So increase of the population will not lead to to a higher standard of living--a more wealthy nation--in and of itself. It may lead to a declining standard of living instead.

On the other hand, an increase in the supply of capital means that each worker has more tools to work with, and can be more productive. That can lead to a higher standard of living--to economic growth.

Discoveries

Thus, investment can be a source of growth. In the long run, probably, discoveries are even more important.

Discovery of new sources of raw materials certainly can lead to a higher standard of living. We can also discover new methods of doing things. The discovery of new methods--

new techniques and technologies--is called "technical progress."

Many students of economic history believe that technical progress is the only source of continuing economic growth in the long run, and that all countries and societies which have experienced rising standards of living over long periods of time (as the European and North American societies have done) have done so because of continuing, and progressive, technological change.

ADAM SMITH ON THE DIVISION OF LABOR

The view of economic growth we have just been discussing is a relatively modern one. Adam Smith had a different view--not necessarily contrary to the modern view, just different. It will be worthwhile to digress a bit and review what the founder of our science had to say about the growth of production.

Like modern economists, Smith believed that the standard of living (the Wealth of a Nation) could rise only if the productivity of labor would rise. For Smith, the most important force leading to a rising standard of living was division of labor.

What most people associate with Adam Smith is the idea of the "invisible hand;" the idea, that is, that free markets restrain prices to some "natural" level and assure the supply of goods and services at the "natural" price.

Indeed Smith's discussion of the "invisible hand" comes quite early in The Wealth of Nations, but it is not the first topic Smith takes up. In Smith's logic, it could not be. The very first topic Smith takes up is the division of labor.

Smith argues that increasing the division of labor increases productivity. In one of the most famous passages in the book, Smith illustrates this tendency by a description of work in a pin factory:

But in the way in which this business is now carried on, not only the whole work is a particular trade, but is divided into a number of branches, of which the greater part are likewise peculiar trades.

One man draws out the wire, another straights it, a fourth points it, a fifth grinds it at the top for receiving the head; to make the head requires two or three distinct operations; to put it on, is a particular business, to whiten the pins is another; it is even a trade by itself to put them in the paper; and the important business of making a pin is, in this manner, divided into about eighteen distinct operations, which, in some manufactories, are all performed by distinct hands, though in some others the same man will sometimes perform two or three of them.

I have seen a small manufactory of this kind where only ten men were employed, and where some of them consequently performed two or three distinct operations.

But though they were very poor, and therefore but indifferently accommodated with the necessary machinery, they could, when they exerted themselves, make among them about twelve pounds of pins in a day. There are in a pound about four thousand pins of a middling size.

Those ten persons, therefore, could make among them upwards of forty-eight thousand pins in a day.

But if they had all wrought separately and independently, and without any of them having been educated to this particular business, they certainly could not each of them have made twenty, perhaps not one pin a day; that is, certainly, not the two hundred fortieth, perhaps not the four thousand eight hundredth part of what they are at present capable of performing, in consequence of a proper division and combination of their different operations.

This passage shows what Smith meant by the division of labor, and by the claim that increasing division of labor increases the productivity of labor. What I want to add is that the division of labor and specialization are aspects of what we might call cooperative production. -

In the pin factory, each worker is taking a different part of the work, and in doing his part he is working along with--co-oper-ating with--the other workers in the pin factory. Each relies on the others for the part he or she does not do. They take different roles in production, and the roles are complementary.

Classical economists of the nineteenth century extended this idea, until Richard Ely, a founder of the American Economic Association, argued that cooperation in production is the primary source of high standards of living. Unfortunately, this vision was lost in the twentieth century. Perhaps it will be recovered in the twenty-first.

Smith's first great insight here is that cooperative production increases productivity. "The division of labor... occasions, in every art, a proportionable increase in the productive powers of labor.... It is the great multiplication of the productions of all the different arts, in consequence of the division of labor, which occasions, in a well-governed society, that universal opulence which extends itself to the lowest ranks of the people." In short, "In civilized society [one] stands at all times in need of the co-operation and assistance of great multitudes,..."

The division of labor into different trades is also an aspect (and perhaps the more important aspect) of the division of labor, according to Smith. "In the lone houses and very small villages which are scattered about in so desert a country as the Highlands of Scotland, every farmer must be butcher, baker and brewer for his own family.... A country carpenter deals in every sort of work that is made of wood...[he] is not only a carpenter, but a joiner, a cabinet maker, and even a carver in wood, as well as a wheelwright, a ploughwright, a cart and waggon maker."

This is in contrast to a more developed region. "Observe the accommodation of the most common artificer or day-laborer in a civilized and thriving country, and you will perceive that the number of people of whose industry a part, though but a small part, has been employed in procuring him his accommodation, exceeds all computation." (By accommodation, here, Smith means not only his residence, but everything he consumes, and the example that Smith gives is his coat). Conversely, the laborer's work usually will contribute, directly or indirectly, to meeting the needs of many others in society.

This division of labor is so characteristic of modern society that we may fail to notice it, as a fish fails to notice the water in which he swims.

It was newer, and thus perhaps more noticeable, in Smith's time. Economists have had little to say about it in the twentieth century--at least, in most of the twentieth century. Just recently, in the 1990's, a number of economists specializing in the study of economic growth have again come to see the division of labor as a key cause of growth in the wealth of nations.

OTHER CAUSES OF INCREASED PRODUCTION

We have said a bit about the first three causes of increased production on the list. What about the other two?

If we have only a certain amount of resources to use, and we discover no new methods for using them, and there is no change in the division of labor and specialization in society, then how can production be increased? The answer is that we might improve the use of the resources we have, in either or both of two ways:

- Put the resources to work where they are more productive and useful; that is, improve the "allocation of resources;" or

- Make increased use of resources that are not now being fully used.

These have been the focus of most of the writing on economics in the twentieth century, and accordingly, they correspond roughly to the two great divisions of twentieth century economics:

- microeconomics and
- macroeconomics

Kinds of Economics

Economics, like other studies, can be broken down into more specialized subfields. The broadest categories are just two: microeconomics and macroeconomics.

In explaining these two terms, it might help to go back in history a bit. The word "economics" is based on Greek roots, but that is a bit of a humbug, since the Greeks didn't have a field of study anything like economics.

The two Greek roots of the word "economics" are oikos--meaning more or less the household or family estate--and nomos, which can mean rules, natural laws or laws made by the government, but which in this case primarily means "wise saws" or "rules of thumb." Thus the book Oikonomia, by the Greek author Xenophon, is probably best translated as "rules of thumb for estate management."

Here's how the word "economics" evolved to its modern use. By the 1600's, the interdependence of people and nations through markets had grown so great that it was necessary for governments to have carefully thought out policies to deal with the markets.

The most common such policy was "mercantilism"--and the essence of mercantilism is to try to sell as much as you can to your neighbors, while limiting what they sell to you, so that they have to pay you in gold. But this policy was criticized by a number of thoughtful scholars, of whom

Adam Smith is the most famous. They were engaged in a new specialization: the study of "rules of thumb for the management of the common political household," which is expressed in the Greek-derived phrase "Political Economy." And that is what the new field was called.

Adam Smith and his immediate successors, the "Classical Political Economists" (as Karl Marx called them) were concerned mostly with the workings of a market economy as a whole. In modern terms, we would say that they were concerned with "macroeconomics." The new Greek root here is, of course, "macro," meaning "big." Macroeconomics is concerned with economic phenomena which are "big" in the sense that the whole is "big" in relation to its parts.

However, beginning in the 1870's, scholarship in economics took a turn toward a much more analytic approach, and economists began to be concerned with the workings of the parts which make up a market economy: with the workings of markets for particular goods and services, the functioning of particular companies, and the determinants of demand on the part of individual consumers. This is now called "micro-economics."

The Greek root "micro," meaning small, tells us that the microeconomist is concerned with economic phenomena which are small in the sense that the parts are small in relation to the whole.

This analytic economics began to see itself (with some reason) as a science, and the term "political" in the phrase "political economy" seemed an embarrassment. So it was dropped, and the ending "-ics," as in physics, was tacked onto the end of "econom," to make it sound more scientific.

The analytic approach was very successful for a time. The macroeconomic approach of the Classical Political Economists never disappeared entirely, but it was (so to say) put on the back burner around 1900. But by 1930--as the Great Depression got well under way--the analytic approach didn't look so good. Many economists felt it was time to go back at least partway to the macroeconomic concerns of the Classical Political Economists. The most famous of these economists is John Maynard Keynes.

By the late 1950's--when Paul Samuelson's seminal economics textbook appeared--it was clear that there was much that was useful and true in both approaches, and that the economics profession had to be committed to both macroeconomics and microeconomics. Thus, it was necessary to have words for the two great divisions of economics.

Of course, most economists specialize in one or the other. In practice, the microeconomist studies the working of markets for particular goods and services, and the interdependencies among these, and the supplies and demands of individual enterprises and consumers. (I should say that the individual enterprises and consumers are abstract, not concrete and specific, individuals, as a rule.

The individual markets may be either abstract or concrete). The macroeconomist studies phenomena which seem to affect or arise from the operation of the market system as a whole: unemployment, inflation, the workings of the monetary system, and the determinants of economic growth

APPLIED FIELDS IN ECONOMICS

Of course, there are a larger number of applied fields in economics. Some of these draw more especially on macroeconomics, some on microeconomics, and some draw on aspects of both.

An important applied field that draws on both microeconomics and macroeconomics is international trade theory. Since this field treats the economic system of a country both as a whole and as a part of a world community of trading nations, it is both macroeconomic and microeconomic. Similarly, urban and regional economics tends to be both microeconomic and macroeconomic, since it treats the economies of regions and cities both as wholes and as parts of a larger interdependent community. Economic development, which studies the economic progress the poorer countries, is largely macroeconomic but has its microeconomic aspects.

Industrial organization is an applied field which concentrates on the operation of individual industries, in a less abstract way, but is mainly a specialization within microeconomics. Similarly, labor economics studies the economics of labor markets, and, while it has some macroeconomic aspects, is mainly a specialization within microeconomics. Agricultural economics and the economics of public utilities and regulation are similarly specializations within microeconomics.

The study of the monetary system and the demand for money are a specialization within macroeconomics, as are the studies of investment, inventories, consumption expenditure, and business fluctuations.

Some subspecializations focus more on method and approach and so can be either macroeconomic or microeconomic, depending on the application. Economic statistics, econometrics, and economic history are cases in point. Somewhat similarly, the economics of the public sector is both macroeconomic and microeconomic because government has functions in both spheres.

Other subspecializations straddle the border of microeconomics and macroeconomics because they draw on one of the two great fields but have applications in the other. The economics of information is a case in point. The methods used in this field of specialization are mostly microeconomic, but the results are widely believed to be important in macroeconomics.

Of course, some subfields belong to microeconomics, and some to macroeconomics, but many overlap these two great subdivisions. Here is a tabular summary of the major subfields:

Micro-economics	Macro-economics	Overlapping
Industrial organization	monetary economics	financial economics
labor economics	investment	international trade theory
agricultural economics	inventories	urban and regional economics
the economics of public utilities and regulation	consumption expenditure	economic development
environmental economics	business fluctuations	econometrics
the economics of information industries		economic history
		economics of the public sector

But now is the time to see how these fields and subfields of economics try to think through their subject matter. How do we study economics?

POSITIVE AND NORMATIVE ECONOMICS

Earlier in the chapter, we distinguished two major kinds of economics: microeconomics and macroeconomics. Now we must consider another great dichotomy: Positive versus normative economics. This is an idea we owe to the great conservative social philosopher and economic theorist and statistician, Milton Friedman.

According to Friedman, positive economics has to do with "what is," while normative economics has to do with "what ought to be." Positive economics is a social science, and as such is subject to the same checks on the basis of evidence as any science. By contrast, normative economics has a moral or ethical aspect, and as such goes beyond what a science can say.

It is true that economics cannot rely on experimental methods to verify its hypotheses, in many cases. (Experimental economics is now a growing field, but still somewhat limited in scope). However, the same is true of some of the sciences, ranging from astronomy to ecology. These are observational sciences, and so is positive economics.

Let us illustrate the distinction--and some of its pitfalls--by an example. A person might say "Everybody ought to be paid the same hourly wage, because it is just that each person should be rewarded in proportion to her labor." This is clearly normative economics--it has to do with what should be.

Now, a "positive" economist might observe that this rule would be inefficient, in the following sense. Some occupations require more training, more effort, or more talent than others; or they are more responsible. If these occupations are better rewarded, they will be better performed, and overall productivity of labor will increase as a result. This increase in productivity will be more than enough to pay the higher wages for the skilled, talented, effortful and responsible occupations, with something left over that might make everyone better off. This is positive economics so far as it goes, and like any proposition of positive science, it might be either true or false.

But suppose it is true, and suppose the "positive" economist goes on to say that, because equal wages are inefficient, wages should not be equalized. That would be normative, not positive economics, and it would be fallacious. The normative economist can respond with perfect logic that justice is more important than a reduction in output which may well be quite modest. There is a hidden assumption, and the assumption is that people "ought" to value production over equality of reward, and there is no logical reason why they should, and some people do not.

What the positive econômist can do is spell out (so far as the evidence and reason permit) the consequences of a rule such as equal pay. This is important, since rules always have consequences that are hard to anticipate, and if we understand the consequences we may want to reconsider our support for the rule. But the rules we propose, and the consequences we are interested in, depend upon our values. Not all consequences are equally important! In the last analysis, positive economics is the servant of normative economics. It is a powerful servant, but a poor master, and "positive" economists who lose sight of this and try to give "scientific" answers to questions of "what ought to be" are not only mistaken but, I believe, ineffective. (I don't believe Milton Friedman ever made that mistake). It is possible for economics to be too "scientific."

Some modern (or postmodern?) economists believe we need a broader approach. In fact, the two-hundred-year tradition is a good deal broader. Let me take a few pages and say a little more about the broader approach.

Reasonable Dialog

"Positive" economists have hoped to put economics on a scientific basis, by confining their attention to issues that can be settled on the basis of observation and evidence. But there are important issues in economics that are not a matter of evidence--normative issues, the definition of terms and even the subject matter of economics itself. But not only that. We know now that even the classical physical sciences (such as physics and chemistry) are not really that simple. Even in the most scientific of fields, terminology has to be defined. Evidence almost always has to be interpreted. The evidence is what it is, but what does it mean? In economics, these issues cannot be swept under the rug. They have to be discussed.

There is always a temptation to say that all this discussion and argument is just "rhetoric," in the bad sense of that word--that one person's opinion is as good as that of another. But opinions are no better than the arguments that support them, and some arguments are better, stronger, sounder than others. In order to draw any unprejudiced conclusions in economics--or in any other field, really--we have to somehow evaluate arguments, and figure out which are better and which are worse. When we evaluate arguments we are practicing critical reasoning.

Philosophers, psychologists and others have studied critical reasoning and there are some pretty well understood guidelines to better and worse arguments.

In my own judgment, one of the best guides to evaluating arguments has come from the philosopher Douglas Walton. These guidelines can be summarized by the phrase reasonable dialog. Reasonable dialog may be defined as an exchange of opinions, questions and answers designed to bring out the reasons for the opinions and to criticize and improve the reasoning of all participants. These objectives define the rules of the conversation.

I have said that economics is a two-hundred year conversation--but what kind of conversation is it? I believe the economics conversation should be a reasonable dialog, and that, for the most part, that is what it has been. In this text, I will try to present economics in this way: as a reasonable dialog.

Although this is not a philosophy text, we will need to spend a few pages on the evaluation of arguments--on critical reasoning--in order to set the stage.

Formal Validity

Every argument begins with some assumptions, and proceeds by some sort of reasoning to a conclusion. If the reasoning is airtight, so that the conclusion has to be true whenever the assumptions are true, then the argument is said to be valid. Here is an example of a valid argument:

EXAMPLE 1A

Socrates is a man.

All men are mortal.

Therefore, Socrates is mortal.

This is a very old example known as a classical syllogism.

Valid arguments are important, especially in a field like mathematics, where the "proof" of a theorem is always a valid argument. But, just because the argument is valid, we cannot be sure that the conclusion is correct. Here is another example of a valid argument:

EXAMPLE 1B

If Princeton is in Greece, then Socrates is alive.

Princeton is in Greece

Therefore, Socrates is alive.

This argument is valid, and yet we know that the conclusion is false. The argument is worthless because it begins from wrong assumptions! This argument is still valid, but it is unsound. We say that an argument is unsound if either 1) it begins from assumptions that are known to be false or 2) it is invalid--based on flawed logic.

But there is a middle ground. Many arguments begin from assumptions that are not known to be either true or false, but are thought probable, and proceed by arguments that are sometimes, but not always, correct, such as statistical arguments. Many real conversations have to rely on arguments of these kinds, arguments that are not airtight.

Defeasible Reasoning

Most important and common arguments are not like valid arguments. They are more like Example 2.

EXAMPLE 2a

Green says:

Most economists are not very good writers.

Maynard is an economist.

Therefore, Maynard probably is not a very good writer.

Even if we accept the first two statements, we could reject the third, if we had reasons to believe that Maynard is an exception to the general rule. The argument is defeasible, which means that while (on the one hand) it is somewhat persuasive as a general matter, nevertheless (on the other hand) it is fallible. We can conceive of a counterargument that could undercut it. Here is an example of an undercutting counterargument:

EXAMPLE 2b

Brown says:

That's not true. Maynard is an exception.

I have read his poetry, and it is extremely fine.

Here Brown argues from personal experience, and the argument undercuts the presumption that Maynard is a poor writer. Now, an undercutting argument does not automatically win. As a rule, an undercutting argument will also be a defeasible argument, which means that it can in turn be undercut. In this case, Brown's argument is fairly weak, since it relies strongly on Brown's personal judgment of the quality of Maynard's poetry; another person, who had also read Maynard's poetry, might undercut Brown's response by offering a contrary opinion. But if Green has not read it, this response would not be available to Green, and Green is at the disadvantage. Let us see another way this dialog might play out:

EXAMPLE 2c

Gold says:

I have read it, too, and I disagree. Maynard's verse has no meter or rhyme--it's quite bad.

Brown says:

Well, that's your opinion. But as a Professor of Literature, with many publications in verse criticism, I can tell you that meter and rhyme are not all there is to poetry. I believe most recognized critics of modern verse would agree with me in pronouncing Maynard's work good.

In example 2c, Gold undercuts Brown's position with, essentially, a "my opinion is as good as your opinion" claim, and Brown attempts in turn to undercut that claim by appealing to her own expert knowledge and a claimed consensus (on standards for judging poetry) in a community of experts. This sort of reason may be very powerful in some contexts (for example, a court of law) and less persuasive in others (for example, in a discussion of laboratory science, where replication of experiments is an important criterion). Whether it will be persuasive in this case depends on how reliable we regard experts in this field as being and whether we believe the claim that Brown's judgment reflects a consensus of experts.

Another Example of Defeasible Reasoning

Here is another, rather homely, example of defeasible reasoning.

EXAMPLE 3

Green says:

I have to drive from Media to West Chester. I'll go by route number 403--In my experience, it's a fast route.

Brown says;

Don't go that way--I read in the Daily Times that the bridge is out and route 403 is closed.

Gold says:

No, not any more--I was that way yesterday, the bridge repairs are complete and the road is open.

The proposition under discussion here is "Route 403 is a fast way from Media to West Chester." Green, who made the claim, supports it with an undated appeal to personal experience which, by itself, is sufficient reason for rational belief in the proposition.

However, Brown undercuts that reason by recent evidence from a reliable public source. Gold, in turn, undercuts the evidence from the second person by a still more recent personal observation. By destroying the credibility of the Brown's undercutting evidence, Gold restores the credibility of Green and of the proposition itself.

These examples illustrate the importance of observation and appeals to evidence in defeasible reasoning. The idea of defeasible reasoning may not sound very good--after all, defeasible is a synonym for "fallible"--until we realize that scientific reasoning is always defeasible, and we know the power of scientific reasoning from our everyday life.

It is a commonplace of basic scientific method that experimental evidence is never quite conclusive--it is always a logical possibility that the next experiments will go differently. Indeed, philosopher John Pollack developed the idea of defeasible reasoning largely to give a stronger basis for the philosophy of science.

Since scientists are aiming at general rules, reasoning from evidence is a very strong kind of reasoning in science. Even a single failed experiment could, in principle, mean that the general rule is wrong.

Example 3 is a more practical one, in which the answer may vary from one time to the next. Because of that, it is important that the reports of observation come from a reliable source (as a local newspaper, cited by Green) or better still personal (Gold) and recent (Gold). This is often a problem in economics, and even more often in business and daily life, and is one of the ways in which we cannot always be scientific in economics. These examples also show is that argument from defeasible reasons is a bit more complex than mathematical argument, or than argument from evidence as understood by science and positive economics. When at least some of the arguments are defeasible, they must be teased out and tested by a process of give and take.

The opposition has to be given its day, and if possible, shown to be wrong. Simply to assert one's position, without considering the opposition, is to take the weaker position. In order to advance knowledge, it is necessary to engage in an ongoing conversation, a conversation with rules and procedures related to its shared purposes: reasonable dialog.

Fallacy of Composition

Let's try applying this approach to economics.

EXAMPLE 4

Green says:

If a tobacco company advertises, its sales will increase.

All tobacco companies advertise.

Therefore, prohibition of advertising would reduce sales of tobacco.

There is an unspoken step, here. Green thinks that the tobacco industry as a whole sells more tobacco than it would sell in the absence of advertising. Let's see how he might respond to that criticism:

Brown says:

Are you sure that the overall sales of tobacco are greater on account of advertising than they would be if tobacco companies did not advertise?

Green says:

If each company sells more, then the total sales must be more, right? It's simple addition?

Brown responds:

Not necessarily. An individual company might be able to sell more by taking customers away from the other companies. But they all can't do that at the same time. It's possible that, when they all advertise, those advertisements just cancel out--leaving the same total sales as before.

Brown has undercut Green's reasoning. This illustrates the fact that Green's argument was and is defeasible. But that doesn't mean that Green was wrong.

Advertising may cancel out or it may not--some nonsmokers may be persuaded to smoke if the industry advertises more--and Green could rescue his argument by giving us some reason to believe that Brown is wrong, and that not all advertising would cancel out. Green would then have undercut Brown's undercutter.

Nevertheless, Green's argument, as he originally stated it, contained a fallacy. It is an important fallacy for economics, too, and is called the fallacy of composition. To commit the fallacy of composition is to reason that what one family or company can (or should) do also can (or should) be done by a whole group of families or companies.

This is a fallacy because it ignores the possibility that the group of families or households may interact (for example, taking away customers from one another) so that the group works differently than an individual does. Since interactions of this kind are very common in economics, the fallacy of composition is one we have to be on the look-out for.

In critical reasoning more generally, the fallacy of composition would be an example of an informal fallacy, that is, reasoning that does not directly violate any rules of logic, but is hasty and inconclusive. One of the objectives of critical reasoning is to find and (if possible) repair informal fallacies.

From the point of view of rational dialog, Brown has done Green a favor, by giving Green an opportunity to make his argument stronger and more conclusive--if in fact it is correct.

But now let's apply these ideas by exploring ideas from one particular school of thought--a key school of thought in twentieth century economics--the Neoclassical Economists.We next explore some of the major schools of thought in economics, to put the Neoclassical School in context. The chapter to follow will discuss the basic ideas of the Neoclassical school in more detail.

SCHOOLS OF THOUGHT IN ECONOMICS

At the beginning of the reasonable dialog of economics, the leaders of the conversation were the "Classical Political Economists," who extended and followed the ideas of Adam Smith. Most of the ideas in this chapter come to us from the Classical Political Economists.

In the next chapter we will review some basic ideas from a more recent, very influential group called the Neoclassical Economists.

As the name "Neoclassical" suggests, their ideas have grown out of the "Classical" ideas, but with some important differences of theme and detail. Ideas from the Neoclassical Economists are especially important for microeconomics. However:

- Classical and Neoclassical Economists are not the only kinds there are. There are also (at least)
  - Keynesian economists (we will talk a lot about them in the Macroeconomics section)

  - o Austrian economists, who believe economics should be a purely deductive, but nonmathema--tical study, and
  - o Marxist economists, who rely on the dialectical method to investigate the world

- There are varieties of opinion among neoclassical and classical economists, and some of them might not agree 100% with the descriptions given here.
- The major orientation of this book is Classical. We suppose that could seem a bit old-fashioned, but we believe it isn't really. The concept of "classical economics" in this book is not meant to be a "fundamentalist" one, but rather a twenty-first century version of that 200-year old approach. That will include a good deal from the neoclassical and Keynesian schools, and this and that from other schools of thought.

All the same, I believe this chapter is a fair beginning summary of the most important approaches to the field, and (most important) a good start on learning what the various schools of thought agree and disagree on--the subject matter of economics.

ECONOMICS AS A CONVERSATION

What is economics? I would like to say that economics is a conversation. It is a conversation that has been going on for over two hundred years.

The conversation includes professional economists, citizens, managers, and others. The conversation began with Adam Smith's book "The Wealth of Nations." Smith's topic was: why do some countries have high standards of living?

Like many long-running conversations, the economics conversation has wandered a bit from one topic to another, and subconversations have split off and rejoined the main stem. What sort of conversation is it? I want to say that, at its best, economics is a "reasonable dialog."

The major orientation of this book is toward Classical Economics. Accordingly, we will define economics as Adam Smith did, as "an enquiry into the nature and causes of the wealth of nations."

We can recognize at least five causes that might lead to greater wealth: increase in the supply of resources, especially through investment; discovery of new techniques of production and new supplies of natural resources, increases in the division of labor, improvements in the allocation of resources, and increased use of the resources already available.

The last two of these will take up most of our pages, because modern economics has a lot to say about them and they correspond roughly to the two great branches of modern economics, microeconomics and macroeconomics. As to methods of investigation, we will try to be as scientific as we can, where scientific answers can be gotten.

But we will put nothing beyond criticism and discussion. Assumptions and definitions of terms should be open to criticism, and carefully chosen in the light of critical reasoning. (In practice, careful definitions of terms are especially important in economics). This broadly critical approach is what we call "reasonable dialog."

Anyway, this hypertextbook will try to present modern economics as an ongoing reasonable dialog, and the product of more than two centuries of reasonable dialog. I hope you will join the conversation, enjoy it, and gain something from it.

The Neoclassical Perspective

The "neoclassical" school of thought has been very influential in all branches of economics, and especially in microeconomics. This chapter reviews some ideas from neoclassical economics which have been adopted throughout much of economics, and which are fundamental for the rest of this book.

Neoclassical Economics

Recall that "improving the allocation of resources" is one of the five ways we might increase the wealth of a nation. "allocation of resources" is a key concept especially for microeconomics, and you will read about it here again and again.

Almost all economists would agree that the allocation of resources is an important aspect of economic thinking and of real economic systems. I say almost all economists--I would like to say all economists would agree to that, but I'm not quite sure there is anything all economists would agree on. Certainly the allocation of resources is important from the point of view of this book.

However, there has been a school of thought in economics in the twentieth century, enormously influential especially in the United States, for which the allocation of resources is more than just one of the considerations. This school of thought is called "neoclassical economics," and the "neo" means that they differ in important ways from the "classical economists" of the previous century.

Neoclassical economists share some of the following points in common.

- For neoclassical economics, economics is the study of the allocation of resources. In this school of thought, economics is defined as "The study that considers human behavior as a relation between scarce means and alternative ends."
- Almost all neoclassical economists are positive economists, though there are some positive economists who are not neoclassical. Thus,

neoclassical economists regard the study of the allocation of resources as essentially a scientific, not a normative, study.

- Neoclassical economists believe that free markets usually bring about an efficient allocation of resources.
- Conversely, efficient allocation is the important thing about free markets. In those more or less rare cases when markets "fail" to bring about an efficient allocation of resources, it is appropriate for the government to intervene to correct the situation, if it can.

With this strong focus on the allocation of resources and on the role of markets, neoclassical economists have indeed learned an enormous amount about these topics, and will have much to teach us.

Neoclassical economists have led the way in clearing up some key concepts almost all economists would rely on. Let us spend a few more pages on topics that--while important to all economists--are especially central for neoclassical economists.

ASSUMPTIONS: RATIONALITY AND SELF-INTEREST

Depending on the definition we prefer, we may say that economists are interested in the allocation of resources, in the nature and causes of the wealth of nations, or perhaps something else.

Regardless, all of those things depend on the actions and decisions of human beings. So, in order to get started, economists are going to have to make some assumptions about human beings, about how human beings act and how human beings decide how to act.

4We might turn to psychology for our assumptions--after all, psychologists are the professionals in the study of the human mind--but in practice, most economists have not done that.

It may be that the theories of psychologists do not answer the questions economists need to ask, or that there are many competing psychological hypotheses, or that economists are stubborn fellows--but, for whatever reason, economists have not as a rule based their assumptions on psychological views of the human mind.

Rather, most economists have begun from an assumption few modern psychologists would endorse. The assumption is that human beings are highly rational and self-interested.

This assumption is especially characteristic of neoclassical economists. Some non-neoclassical economists do also accept it, but some do not.

Neoclassical economists usually assume, in other words, that human beings make the choices that give them the best possible advantage, given the circumstances they face. Circumstances include the prices of resources, goods and services, limited income, limited technology for transforming resources into goods and services, and taxes, regulations, and similar objective limitations on the choices they may make.

I should modify that a little right away. Strictly speaking, neoclassical economics does not assume that real, concrete human beings are rational and self-interested.

Rather, most economists assume that economic systems work as if they consisted of rational, self-interested persons. After all, it is averages that count for these purposes.

People are of all sorts; sneaky and altruistic, smart and dumb, but if the average is a person who is rational and self-interested, then the system will "act as if" people in general were rational and self-interested. At least, that is the basis of "neoclassical" economics: it is assumed that deviations from rational self-interest are random and will cancel out and so the system will act as if everyone were rational and self-interested. Accordingly, neoclassical economics studies an economic system consisting of rational, self-interested persons.

We should pause a little further over these assumptions before moving on. They are not particularly common-sense assumptions. We all know of examples of non-self-interested behavior--of people who give to the church and to good causes and who sacrifice themselves in other ways--and my common sense (at least) suggests to me that people are often irrational chumps.

Assumptions: Rationality and Self-Interest

There are two very different issues here. The first issue is that people are sometimes altruistic. It is hard to avoid the conclusion that people do sometimes act on ethical values , and it is hard to see how the selfishness of the (probable) majority can "cancel out" this self-sacrifice.

It seems that we really have to modify the assumption of self-interest in order to accommodate the evidence. People often do act on non-self-interested values--but when they do so they act on their own values, not those of the government, some philosopher, or (most important) the observing economist.

We might call this assumption "rational individualism" rather than "rational self interest." But, as it turns out, it doesn't make much difference for the theory , except to make it more complicated. We shall avoid the complications here by adopting the analysis based on self-interest.

What, then, is left of rationality if people are not always self-interested? A broader (but still neoclassical) neoclassical economics assumes that people choose in the way that best advances their own values, altruistic or self-interested as those values may be.

The suspicion that people are often irrational might be easier to deal with, since it is at least possible that deviations from rationality could be random and could cancel out.

If they are not, then we may be able to make some adjustments as we go along. In fact, there is a good deal of evidence that real choices can deviate from rationality in predictable ways. To the extent that they do, we can understand their choices in two stages: first, understand what the rational choices would be, and, second, adjust that for any predictable irrationality. (Some economists will feel that the second step isn't necessary, but we can take the first step together).

This leads us back to the the distinction of positive and normative economics. Critics of neoclassical economics sometimes claim that economics is an apology for self-interest; that economics, like Gordon Gekko, holds that "greed is good."

This is a misunderstanding. The assumption of rational self-interest is positive economics, an attempt to describe what is, not what ought to be. But is it true? That is the criterion for positive economics, and we shall have to return to the question from time to time.

Assumptions and Critical Reasoning

But the assumptions of rationality and self-interest may not really be questions of fact. I believe they make more sense if we think of them as guidelines for critical reasoning in economics.

Take the assumption of rationality, for example. When we observe that other people disagree with use, or that they do things we would not do in their place or that we would rather they not do, it is very easy to say that they are irrational.

This is a fallacy, since I could just as easily be the irrational one--if anybody is irrational--and there could be many other reasons why we disagree. By starting from the assumption that people are rational, and trying to explain the disagreements on the basis of rationality--not irrationality--I protect myself from that fallacy. Just because I start with the assumption of rationality doesn't mean I have to stick with it, and sometimes I don't; but it proves right more often than not, so it is the right place to begin a study of economics.

The assumption of self-interest works somewhat the same way. It may seem very cynical always to try to explain human behavior first in terms of self-interest--but what is the alternative? When we assume self-interested motives we are reasoning as follows:

"Self-interested motives are common among human beings.

Joe Smith is a human being.

Therefore, it is probable that Joe Smith's motives in this particular case are self-interested."

Experience teaches us that self-interested motives are indeed pretty common. There are exceptions, I believe, and that means the rule "Human beings are self-interested" is a defeasible rule. It's a good guideline for critical reasoning in economics, but we have to be aware that there are exceptions.

I believe almost all modern economists would accept these assumptions as guidelines for sound critical reasoning in economics, if not as facts.

For now, however, let us look at some less controversial points from the neoclassical economists, points that will be important for all modern economists:

- the key role of scarcity in economics, and
- the use of models as a means of exploring that and other economic topics.

MODELS IN ECONOMICS

Of course, the real world of economics is very complex. The allocation of resources in a market economy is the result of the interaction of thousands of decisions made by each of hundreds of millions of individual people. Economics deals with this complexity in part by thinking in terms of "models."In a modern economic system, individuals, companies, markets and even nations are interdependent.

A model (of a particular subsystem of the economic system) is a description of these interdependencies in terms of mathematics, pictures, a computer programming language, or some similar descriptive language, together with a theory of the dynamics of the subsystem. Dynamics is the way the subsystem evolves as time passes.

Models are usually somewhat more complex than theories, and a theory may be just one part of a model. Like theories, however, models are abstract, and must ignore some aspects of the system they describe.

The term "model" is sometimes used in two different ways. The most common usage in economics can be expressed as "a model of." This is the usage just described: a "model of" is descriptive. However, we may also hear of a "model for," as in "the economy of Taiwan provides a model for all of China to emulate." In economics, "model of" is the primary meaning, and nothing more will be said here about "models for."

In economics, a model is most likely to take the form of a list of variables and one or more relationships among the variables. These variables and relationships describe the interdependence among the people and activities in the economic system or subsystem, and the way these activities change as time passes.

Examples serve best to make this clear. In the next few sections, we will illustrate this approach by discussing a model of a very basic economic concept, the concept of "scarcity." This model is one we use in discussing the allocation of resources, so we will come back to it in studying microeconomics, and it will illustrate the key role of allocation of resources in modern economics, as well as giving an example of economic models.

SCARCITY

Resources of all kinds are scarce. That simply means that we do not have enough resources to produce all of the goods and services that anybody might like to have. It means that we, as a society, must somehow answer some basic questions: What resources will be used to produce which goods and services.

To answer these questions, and get the resources to the users, is to "allocate" resources. We would, of course, like to organize things so that the resources are used for the most urgent and rewarding kinds of production--that is, we would like to allocate resources "efficiently."

In the Soviet Union, under the system of economic planning, the allocation of resources was pretty obvious--the government decided who got to use which resources. The government "allocated resources" in a way that anyone would recognize. (They don't seem to have done it very efficiently, though). Notice, however, that markets also allocate resources.

This allocation is not as obvious--it goes on while we are not looking, so to say--so we don't always think of it as allocation. But it is allocation of resources, since the bidding and higgling and haggling and deal-making of the market-place does determine which resources are used for what purposes.

A Model Illustrating Scarcity, Part I

Let's have an example of a model in economics. At the same time, it will be a model that illustrates what economists mean by scarcity. The model we shall use for our example is the Production Possibility Frontier model. To repeat, scarcity and choice go hand in hand.

This has far-reaching implications. Productive resources are always scarce, since we cannot increase the output of one kind of product without decreasing that of another. Of course, our economy produces many kinds of goods and services, so that we may be able to understand that better if we think in terms of a model. For our model, let us think of an economy that produces just two kinds of goods: "machines" and food.

At any given time, a country cannot produce more machines without producing less of something else. (In this case, the country produces less food). Table below shows, for the model country, how much food they can produce given each respective output of machines. For example, to increase machine output from 7000 to 8000, they would have to cut food output from 1020 to 720.

Table

machines	*food*
0	2000
1000	1980
2000	1920
3000	1820
4000	1680
5000	1500
6000	1280
7000	1020
8000	720
9000	380
10000	0

This relationship is called the "production possibility frontier."

Let's be sure you understand how to read the table. It tells us, for example, that when the economy produces 3000 machines, it can produce 1820 units of food. To increase machine production to 4000, it would be necessary to reallocate resources from the production of food to the production of machines. This will reduce the production of food; the table tells us that it would reduce the production of food to 1680.

A Model Illustrating Scarcity, Part II

Many models in economics can be expressed by diagrams. Here is a diagram of the production possibility frontier in the table on the previous page. A combination of food and machines is said to be "feasible" if the economy has enough resources to produce both.In the figure, all feasible combinations of food and machinery are on or underneath the curve. Combinations above the curve are not feasible--there is not enough resources to produce that much of both.

Demonstration of the Production Possibilities Frontier

Let's try an exercise to test your understanding. Try clicking on the diagram, first on feasible and then on infeasible combinations.

3

The Economics of Money Laundering Enforcement

The paper shows how excessive reporting, called "crying wolf", can dilute the information value of reports. Excessive reporting is investigated by undertaking the first formal analysis of money laundering enforcement. Banks monitor transactions and report suspicious activity to government agencies, which use these reports to identify investigation targets. Banks face fines should they fail to report money laundering. However, excessive fines force banks to report transactions which are less suspicious. The empirical evidence is shown to be consistent with the model's predictions. The model is used to suggest implementable corrective policy measures, such as decreasing fines and introducing reporting fees.

INTRODUCTION

Money laundering gained notoriety: The FBI (2001) estimates money laundering volumes up to $1,500 billion.

Furthermore, terrorists have joined the ranks of money launderers increasing national security concerns. Responding to that, law enforcement agencies paid increasing attention to money laundering offenses. Most importantly, they required banks to report and identify suspicious activities, and threatened with fines if they fail to do so. Banks responded by exploding the number of reports, and many times they report innocent activities. The Wall Street Journal (2004a), for example, covers the case of the falsely reported former presidential candidate and Senate majority leader Bob Dole. The question of the paper is: Is this reporting system efficient? And if not, how could it be made more efficient?

The paper shows formally how excessive reporting in this situation fails to identify what is truly important by diluting the information value of reports. The intuition can be best understood through an analogy with the tale: "The boy who cried wolf". In the tale, the boy cried wolf so often, that his cries became meaningless. Similarly, excessive reporting, which will be referred to as "crying wolf", fails to identify what is truly relevant. This crying wolf problem will be shown to be relevant in other economic situations, such as product information and auditing as well. More generally, the model shows that information is not only data, but also able and expert identification of truly important data.

The reporting problem is investigated through the first formal analysis of money laundering enforcement. Choosing money laundering enforcement as the leading example is motivated by the fact that the identification role of reports is particularly strong. Furthermore, money laundering is an economically significant crime. Several hundred billion dollars are washed through the financial sector in the United States, and money laundering facilitates crimes as harmful as drug trafficking and terrorism, as detailed in the next section.

The model explores the agency problem between the bank and government law enforcement agencies. The bank monitors transactions and reports suspicious activity to the government, which identifies targets for investigations based on these reports. The bank undertakes costly monitoring and reporting, because the government fines it if money laundering is successfully prosecuted and the bank did not report the transaction. Though Masciandaro (1999) abstracted from this agency problem in the first economic analysis of money laundering, it is crucial as the later survey by Masciandaro and Filotti (2001) shows.

The formal model builds on five main economic building blocks. First, communication is coarse between the bank and the government, as the bank cannot communicate in a short report all the local information it has. This communication problem is similar in spirit to the information hardening problem in Stein (2002), though here the problem is not with verifying the information, but rather with telling it precisely. Second, the bank's incentives to report are coarse; the bank is fined only for false negatives, i.e. for not reporting transactions which are prosecuted later as money laundering. Third, the bank is always uncertain about the transaction's true nature, i.e. every transaction can be potential money laundering. Fourth, the bank faces dual tasks: it has to monitor all transactions in order to report the suspicious ones. Fifth, the bank's information, i.e. its signal on the transaction, is not verifiable ex-post, because the local information at the time of the judgment cannot be reproduced later.

The model shows that harmful excessive reporting, called crying wolf, can arise in this setup. As the bank cannot share its signal with the government, the government must make decisions based on whether or not it observes the report. Intuitively, if the bank identifies all transactions as suspicious, then it fails to identify any one of them-exactly as if it would not have identified a single one. Thus, crying wolf can fully eliminate the information value of reports. Crying wolf can arise because excessively high fines for false negatives force the uncertain bank to err on the safe side and report transactions which are less suspicious. In the extreme case the bank is forced to report all transactions, thereby fully diluting the information value of reports.

The paper shows that the model's findings are consistent with the available empirical evidence in the United States. Fines have increased in the last ten years, especially so after the USA Patriot Act. In response, banks have reported an increasing number of transactions. However, the number of money laundering prosecutions has fallen-even though the estimates of money laundering volumes have been stable. Furthermore, regulatory agencies have identified 'defensive filing' which exhibits striking similarities with what happens under crying wolf.

The model also provides implementable policy implications on how to stop crying wolf and thereby increase the efficiency of money laundering enforcement. First, the model calls for reduced fines to cease crying wolf, as optimal and not maximal fines are needed. The bank needs some fines in order to monitor and report, but excessively strong ones result in crying wolf. The intuition behind deviating from Becker's (1968) seminal proposal of maximal deterrence is that banks are not criminals, but rather honest informants. Thus, excessively strong incentives do not deter banks from committing a crime, but rather distort their information provision.

Second, reporting fees might be needed to elicit optimal reporting. As in Holmström and Milgrom (1991), single dimensional incentives might not be able to elicit efficient two-dimensional banking effort to monitor and report. Reporting fees provide an implementable second dimension of incentives by punishing the bank for false positives. Furthermore, reporting fees can be thought of as pricing reporting externalities. Each report dilutes the value of all other reports, and reporting fees would make banks internalize these externalities.

Third, the model's most important comparative static result shows that fines should decline in the harm caused by money laundering. The intuition is that the bank's effective incentives have two components: government investigation to identify false negatives and nominal fines. As money laundering becomes more harmful, optimal government investigation increases as the marginal benefit of prosecuting money laundering increases. However, the bank's incentives should be constant so as not to trigger crying wolf. Thus, the model shows that the fine increase of the USA Patriot Act, which reacted to the new threat of terrorism and terrorism financing, could have been intuitive, but mistaken measure.

As it was argued earlier, crying wolf is a general economic problem. The main economic building blocks identified in money laundering enforcement can be found in many other situations. For instance, product information provision is very similar to suspicious activity reporting. Firms must use their expertise to identify the most relevant dangers related to using their product. There, coarse incentives are provided by the legal structure: omissions of warnings can result in damages and following lawsuits. False positives have no such easily identifiable victims. However, there is a real damage from crying wolf, because information is lost, as customers disregard warnings and accept contracts without reading the fine print.

The agency setup of the model is very similar to that of the auditing problems analyzed first in Tirole (1986). The government uses both auditors and banks to obtain information about their clients. More precisely, the government is interested in learning if there are problems such as accounting omissions or signs of money laundering. Naturally, both auditors and banks are reluctant to provide such negative information, which creates an agency problem.

These similarities in the agency setup allow building on the Kofman and Lawarrée (1993) auditing model in setting up the action set. A major difference from the crying wolf problem is, however, that the auditing literature focused on the disclosure of verifiable or certifiable information as reviewed in Verrecchia (2001).

The model's focus on coarse communication of unverifiable information is particularly relevant to investigate the increased role of auditors after the Sarbanes-Oxley Act. Auditors are not only supposed to disclose verifiable information, but they also have to identify material transactions, i.e. transactions that fundamentally affect the firm's value. Identifying material transactions is very similar to identifying suspicious activities, because in both cases unverifiable and uncertain information is identified through coarse communication. Furthermore, auditors are also sanctioned for false negatives, i.e. for not disclosing transactions which later substantially affect the firm's value. Thus, excessive fines might make auditors report more transactions as material, thereby failing to identify the truly important ones. Lengthening auditing reports and firm disclosures, documented in Gordon (2005), might well signal crying wolf.

The model can be extended to various other settings. The model questions the understanding in corporate finance that more disclosure is always better, which could be tested empirically following La Porta et al. (2006). A particularly interesting application of the crying wolf problem can arise in intelligence settings following the research started in Garicano and Posner (2005).

MONEY LAUNDERING ENFORCEMENT

Money laundering is defined as an illicit money transfer. There are two main kinds of illicit money transfers. First, traditional money laundering entails transferring illegally obtained funds to conceal their origins and make them appear legal. For example, drug dealers deposit cash revenues in banks and later transfer them until the funds appear to originate from legitimate sources. Second, terrorism financing entails transferring mostly legal funds for illegal purposes.

For instance, legal charity donations are transferred to fund terrorist attacks. In sum, both forms of money laundering are characterized by illicit and socially harmful fund transfers. Money laundering causes social harm because it facilitates crime and enables criminals to enjoy criminal revenues.

Money laundering can happen through various intermediaries. Bank transfers, both by wire and check, are the most common channels for illicit money transfers as described in Reuter and Truman (2004). Money transmitting businesses, such as Western Union, are also used for money laundering as detailed in The Wall Street Journal (2004b).

These businesses are typically franchised or owned by individuals, who might have stronger incentives to turn a blind eye to money laundering than bank branch-managers. In the greyer area of finance, informal value transfer systems (IVTSs) provide money transmitting services usually without a proper paper trail. The hawala or hindi systems used by different ethnic communities are described, for instance, in El-Qorchi (2002).

Money laundering is an economically significant crime, though precise estimates are hard to obtain. According to Camdessus (1998), the consensus range of money laundering volume is between 2 and 5 percent of the global GDP. The FBI (2001) estimates the volume of globally laundered funds as falling between $600 billion and $1.5 trillion.

Laundering fees, i.e. what money launderers charge their criminal clients, are estimated at 5-15% of the laundered amount according to Lal (2003) and Reuter and Truman (2004). Thus, money laundering, including self-laundering, is estimated to be a $30 to $225 billion global 'industry'. Moreover, the harm caused for instance by terrorism financing shows that money laundering is potentially even more significant than what volumes and laundering revenues would suggest. Money laundering enforcement is particularly relevant for the United States.

According to some lawmakers' estimates, half of the globally laundered funds are transferred through US Banks (FBI, 2001). Three known money laundering cases highlight the point. First, $7 billion of Russian funds were washed through the Bank of New York until 1999 (Reuter and Truman, 2004).

Responding to the threat of money laundering, the United States has developed one of the strongest anti-money laundering regulation. The Banking Secrecy Act (1970), which in fact curbed banking secrecy to fight money laundering, was followed by a series of laws, each one of them further strengthening money laundering enforcement: The Money Laundering Control Act (1986), the Annunzio-Wylie Money Laundering Act (1992), the Money Laundering Suppression Act (1994), The Money Laundering and Financial Crimes Strategy Act (1998) and finally the USA Patriot Act (2001).

Second, Stephen Saccoccia alone laundered up to $550 million of drug money for both the Calí and Medellin cartels until he was prosecuted in 1993 (Reuter and Truman, 2004). Third, terrorists transferred $0.5 million for the 9/11 attack (9/11 Commission Report, 2004). The examples also show that the volumes involved in laundering proceedings of tax evasion and drug trafficking are enormous compared to terrorism financing.

Money laundering enforcement relies on bank reporting to law enforcement and government agencies as reviewed in Reuter and Truman (2004). Banks provide two kinds of reports: rule-based and discretionary reports. For instance, banks file the rule-based currency transaction report (CTR) for any cash transactions exceeding $10,000. Enforcing rule-based reporting is a standard disclosure problem as bank actions are ex-post verifiable. They are, however, insufficient, because money launderers are aware of the rules and can circumvent them.

For instance, money launderers usually 'smurf', i.e. break down large cash deposits over $10,000 into smaller deposits below the reporting threshold. Nevertheless, rule-based reporting makes money laundering more cumbersome.

The weaknesses of rule-based reports led to the introduction of a discretionary report, the suspicious activity report (SAR), in 1996. The suspicious activity report is filed for any activity that the bank considers to be 'suspicious'. For instance, if the bank spots several transactions just below $10,000, it can identify them as suspicious because they hint at smurfing.

The notion of suspicion is intentionally left vague so as to leave both money launderers and banks uncertain. Thus, money launderers cannot rely on simple rules to avoid being reported. Furthermore, banks are forced to constantly improve their understanding of how money laundering is done.

This intentional vagueness can be understood as another form of constructive ambiguity. The SARs are filed to the Financial Crime Enforcement Network (FinCEN), which might forward them to law enforcement agencies for further investigation.

Banks incur costly screening, monitoring and reporting because of the threat of sanctions.

Failing to file SARs led to fines of $25 million for Riggs Bank (FinCEN, 2004a), $24 million for Arab Bank (FinCEN, 2005f), $50 million for AmSouth Bank (FinCEN, 2004b) and $80 million for ABN-AMRO Bank (FinCEN, 2005g). Most importantly, sanctions or fines are levied for false negatives, i.e. for not reporting transactions which are later prosecuted as money laundering or judged to be suspicious ex-post.

Banks are not fined for false positives, i.e. for reporting legal transactions as money laundering. This 'safe harbor' provision strengthens banks incentive to report.

MODEL SETUP

The model explicitly investigates the agency problem between the government and the bank, where the government needs information from the bank to investigate the transaction which may or may not be money laundering. If the bank monitors the transaction, then it receives information, a signal about the transaction. The informed bank, which has received the signal is able to inform the government by filing a suspicious activity report. The government provides incentives, by means of fines, for the bank to monitor and report suspicious transactions.

4

Money and Banking

THE CONCEPT OF MONEY AND ITS FUNCTIONS

The topics of this chapter are covered by the text taken from the book: Henderson & Poole: Principles of Economics p. 813-850. The only topic we add here to the material taken from Henderson & Poole is a short history of money.

A Short History of Money

In the history of money, various periods have occurred1. At the time when money was not invented, the relative values of goods were expressed in the units of the two goods bartered with each other. For example, a certain amount of cotton was exchanged for a negotiated amount of salt. Gradually certain goods were started to be used as measurement units for the values of other goods. This way was invented the first goods money. Examples are corn, cattle, fur, various metals and in Africa even cocoa. In Finnish language, the original meaning of the term money was squirrel fur.

The benefits of precious metals as compared with other goods money were:

(1) *Transportability*: great intrinsic value related to size and weight,

(2) *Divisibility*: "money" could be used in small exchanges too,

(3) *Homogeneity*: the quality of "money" need not be checked,

(4) *Stability of value*: in some transactions the medium of exchange needed to be stored for some time during which its value should stay constant.

Precious metals fulfilled the above criteria better than for instance fur and corn, which explained their gained popularity with time. The first metal money was invented most probably around 600 (b.c.) in Asia Minor. The transportation, storing and division of precious metal money was not easy, however. Due to these reasons, paper money such as bank notes and checks, started to pass over the precious metal money as the medium of exchange. In a precious metal based monetary system, bank notes were so called representative money.

The one who had issued the bank note (who had written the receipt for the depositor of gold or silver) has promised to return the gold to the owner of the receipt (note) at full value. In this way the notes represented the amount of gold or silver stored in some organization, which thereafter were started to be called banks.

The first such organizations were Goldsmiths, who needed the metals as raw material for their products. Later on some Goldsmiths started to concentrate more on their deposit business, and they were the predecessors of banks. The advantage of bank notes as compared with precious metals were that the 'deposited' gold or silver was not needed to be transported from one person to another for the payment; only the owner of the receipt was changed in the exchange and the precious metal stayed safely in the "bank account".

When the exchange of goods increased in Europe at the beginning of the 1700'th century, the payment system was centered in great trading houses called Giro banks. Giro banks accepted precious metals as deposits to strike coins from these metals, and gave a receipt from these "deposits" to the depositors. These receipts were used as a means of payments of goods (a medium of exchange), and so they were the first bank notes. Giro banks were the predecessors of currently existing central banks, which have a unanimous right to issue bank notes. At the 1800'th century in various countries there were by side with precious metal money also bank notes circulating with limited use; they were accepted only locally. Gradually the public authorities took itself the uniform right to issue bank notes, and this way money started to lose its meaning as a good. In Finland, the Bank of Finland has had the unanimous right to issue money since 1886.

In nowadays existing paper standard monetary systems, bank notes are not redeemed by gold or silver. Modern notes are pure paper money (fiat money), and their value is based on people's general trust on their current and future purchasing power. The change from precious metal based monetary systems to paper based monetary systems was a remarkable one, although in practice they function in an identical way. In paper standard monetary systems notes and coins are the principal medium of exchange. The next innovation in the means of payments was the invention of checks. Check is a medium of exchange which is related to the bank account of the writer of the check.

Definition: Check is a request to pay to the holder of the check a written amount of money from the account of the writer of the check. _ The advantage of checks as compared with bank notes is the smaller need to hold cash money. This decreases the risk of losing money or being robbed. The newest forms of the medium of exchange are bank and credit cards, which work essentially in the same way as checks. Their advantage as compared with checks is a smaller transaction cost. Another advantage is the gained interest returns due to keeping money on a bank account rather than on a checking account, which offers lower interest rate.

The disadvantage related to bank and credit cards is the uncertainty of the buyers' ability to pay. Various banks have guaranteed-the payments made by their bank cards up to a certain limit. The reason for this is that the bank has the best information about the credibility of its clients.

A characteristic feature of a paper money standard is the covering system. At the early stages of the paper money system, gold coverage was 100 %. This means that the gold reserves in banks were equal to the total value of bank notes circulating at every time moment. Gradually bankers begin to realize that they did not have to keep the whole deposited gold in their bank vaults, because of the low probability that all depositors would simultaneously come to redeem their gold. This way was invented the so called fractional reserve banking principle, where banks keep in their vaults only a certain fraction of their deposits, and use most of their deposits to formulate loans for their clients.

In a gold standard paper money system, the amount of money circulating can exceed the gold reserves of the central bank by a certain amount so that only a part of the aggregate nominal value of bank notes circulating is covered by gold. In Finland, the rules of the Bank of Finland define the quality of assets and the minimum required coverage of bank notes circulating. The aggregate number of bank notes circulating at a certain moment of time depends on the central bank's monetary policy and on the economic policy of the public sector.

According to this section, we can divide different monetary systems into two categories on the basis of whether the exchange value of one unit of currency corresponds to its value in use. These two classes are: goods money and symbolic money. If the exchange value of some goods money (for instance squirrel fur) does not correspond to its value in use, it is worth for the owner of the money to use it himself. On this basis, the exchange value of a goods money is always greater than or equal to its value in use. If the value of the metal in a coin is greater than the purchasing power of the coin, it is profitable to melt the coin and sell the metal (which though is illegal in Finland). On the other hand, the exchange value of every symbolic money (for example a bank note) always exceeds its value in use, and symbolic money is applicable only when its issuing and its amount in circulation is controlled.

When the world wide depression occurred in the beginning of 1930's, various countries had to give up the gold standard. The gold reserves in the Bank of England diminished during the 1920's so much that England had to give up the gold standard at 1931. This devalued the pound sterling, which affected the whole world's payment system. The international banking and payment system is highly integrated in the way that a bank panic in one major banking center affects the payment system of the whole world. Due to the problems in England, various other European countries, including all Scandinavian countries, had to give up their gold standard. Bank of Finland stopped redeeming its bank notes with gold at 1931. It was believed at that time that giving up of the gold standard is a temporary phenomena, but it has turned permanent. The current monetary system in Finland, and in almost every western economy, is so called free monetary system or a paper money system.

Definition: Monetary system of a country covers all laws and regulations related to the legal means of payments in the country.

Definition: We call money, or legal tender, the legal medium of exchange which every participant in the corresponding economy is obligated to accept.

Definition: Essentially two forms of legal tender exists: Principal money (notes) and exchange money (coins). Every one has to accept principal money as a medium of exchange, but exchange money need to be accepted only up to a small amount. The official supplier of legal tender, the corresponding central bank, has to accept also exchange money without any limit.

The transformation from a gold standard paper money system to a paper money system is made so that the public authority declares the central bank notes as the legal medium of exchange. This means that money loses its value as a good, and so there is not any more a fixed correspondence between one unit of paper money and a certain amount of precious metal. In a paper money system, the internal purchasing power as well as the external exchange rate of the currency varies more than in a precious metal standard monetary system. If then the central bank can freely change the foreign exchange rates of the currency, the system is called a free paper money standard. If, on the other hand, the foreign exchange rates are kept fixed for instance via agreements concerning international trade or policy, the system is called a binding paper money standard.

The International Monetary Fund (IMF) was founded together with the International Bank for Reconstruction and Development (World Bank) in a meeting in Bretton Woods at 1945. Finland became a member of IMF at 1948. IMF has had a central role in the negotiations concerning the development of the international payment system. At the beginning, the exchange rates between currencies of countries belonging in the IMF were defined on gold basis. This monetary system was called gold parity standard. According to this system, a gold standard existed between the central banks of countries belonging in IMF, although the monetary systems of member countries were not based on gold standard. The member countries-which were the majority of all countries-did not have a right to change the fixed exchange rates of their currency with respect to other currencies without the permission of IMF more than 10 %. The idea of this agreement was to decrease the observed variability of exchange rates.

THE ADVANTAGES OF A MONETARY SYSTEM

In various markets we can observe direct and indirect exchanges. A direct exchange (a bilateral barter) means that two goods are exchanged with each other without any external medium of exchange. In a direct barter, we cannot identify which one of the two "trading" partners is the buyer and which is the seller, because both parties use the two exchanged goods themselves. Ancient economies were based on the bilateral bartering of goods. For example, agricultural products were exchanged for salt and cotton etc.

Sometimes in a bilateral barter, the partners have to accept as a means of payment goods which they do not use themselves, which they must further barter to get such goods they need. In these cases we can identify the seller and the buyer in the exchange: the one who accepts goods he will not use himself as a means of payment is the seller and the other the buyer of the good. An economic system based on bilateral barter is very inefficient, because the needs of two people seldom meet exactly, and it takes time to find people with suitable needs for the barter. For example, a farmer willing to use dentist services has to find a dentist who accepts carrots as a means of payment, or he has first to exchange carrots to such products his dentist likes to be paid with.

The lack of money in a barter economy creates two kinds of transaction costs: searching costs for finding trading partners and transportation costs for the goods bartered. The third indirect cost is that there exists exchange operations of which all involved would benefit, which are impossible in a barter economy. Suppose, for example, that a French wine farmer likes Iranian carpets. The owners of the carpets are muslims, however, who do not drink wine. This means that a third partner should be found who likes wine and produces such goods muslims like to have.

The benefits from indirect exchange are greatest when such of a good can be found which every partner in the market accepts as a means of making payments, that is, the money. The invention of money for the medium of exchange dramatically improved the efficiency of the exchange of goods. It made possible various exchanges impossible in barter economies, and it also decreased the transaction costs in every exchange. The above described advantages of the use of a generally accepted medium of exchange were so obvious that even in ancient times people started to use some specific goods as a medium of exchange.

Besides money, also other ways exist to solve the pricing and payment problems in a multilateral barter. Suppose that a central authority exists who collects the bids of every good and sets the relative "prices" of every two goods so that the demands of every participant are met. These relative prices need to be accepted by every participant, which would lead to a complicated negotiation between the partners. The complexity of this kind of a multilateral barter increases with the number of participants and the number of goods, which makes it very clumsy in practice. Imagine, for example, the re-calculation of every price with the occurring of new bids etc. Due to these reasons, multilateral barter systems are met quite seldom in practice. A centralized trading system can take place when the goods traded are highly standardized and the confidence of every participant is guaranteed. Examples of such are stock and raw material exchanges which function on an auction principle.

PRINCIPLES OF BANKING AND CENTRAL BANKING

Fundamentals of Financial Markets

Definition: We call financial markets the markets where surplus funds (savings) of economic units such as firms, households, government, local government and foreign investors, are channelled to those economic units who have a shortage of funds, that is, to those who like to borrow funds. We call direct finance the borrowers' borrowing of funds directly from the lenders who sell them securities (financial instruments), which are claims on the borrowers' future income or assets. While securities are assets for the person who buys them, they are liabilities for the individual or firm that sells or issues them. For example, if General Motors needs to borrow funds in order to build a new factory, it can directly borrow funds from a saver by selling him a bond.

Definition: A Portfolio is the collection of securities owned by a certain economic unit.

The reason that securities are called financial instruments is that various securities can be used as "instruments" by which investors can affect the risk and return (yield) combination of their portfolio. Because every asset in one portfolio has a specific yield and risk combination, then changing the content of the portfolio affects its aggregate return and risk.

Why is this channelling of funds from savers to those who spend important for an economy? The answer is that those who save are frequently not the same people who have profitable investment opportunities. Suppose that you have saved $ 1000, you have no investment opportunity for that money, and there are no financial markets in the economy. Then you will keep the money in your pocket, no-one can use your money for investment and you will not get interest earnings on it. Suppose then that a firm exists with a safe profitable investment opportunity which is willing to borrow your $ 1000 and pay it back after one year with an annual interest rate of 5 (%/year).

In this case you would get a compensation for not using your savings, and a profitable investment opportunity in the economy will be financed too. The introduction of financial markets, where the demand of loans and supply of savings meet, is thus a Pareto improvement for the economy (it improves the welfare of some person(s) without decreasing that of others) as compared with the situation that such markets do not exist.

Another example for the importance of financial markets is housing loans. A person who does not own wealth but has a regular salary can get a mortgage loan from financial markets to buy a house. Without financial markets, only a few of us could buy a house and there would not exist lively housing markets in an economy. This last example also shows the importance of a collateral in the lending business. Definition: A collateral is a general term for various kinds of property offered by the borrower to assure his repayment of his loan.

THE FUNCTIONS OF FINANCIAL INTERMEDIARIES

Funds from lenders to borrowers can move besides directly also indirectly. We call this indirect finance and it involves a middleman called a financial intermediary.

Definition: A financial intermediary borrows money from the lenderssavers and then, in turn, makes loans to the borrowers-spenders.

Financial intermediaries are: 1) depository institutions, 2) contractual savings institutions, and 3) investment intermediaries.

Depository institutions are: 1) commercial banks, 2) savings and loan associations, 3) mutual savings banks, and 4) credit unions.

Contractual savings institutions are: 1) life insurance companies, 2) pension funds, and 3) fire and casualty insurance companies.

Investment intermediaries are: 1) mutual funds, 2) money market mutual funds, and 3) finance companies.

A bank can acquire funds by issuing a liability to the public in the form of savings deposits, and formulate financial assets (instruments) from these funds by issuing loans. For example, a bank can give a loan to General Motors or buy a GM bond from the primary financial market. The ultimate result from this is that funds have been transferred from the public (the lenders-savers) to GM (the borrowerspender) with the help of the financial intermediary (the bank). By charging a higher interest rate on loans than they pay on the funds they acquire (the interest differential), financial intermediaries make profit. Financial intermediaries improve the efficiency of financial markets. The reasons are the following:

(1) People's small savings can get a higher interest rate when they are marketed as a part of a larger loan.

(2) Households and small firms, for which it would be impossible to get funds as direct finance, can get relatively large loans from banks.

(3) Financial intermediaries reduce the costs of collecting information of all borrowers and lenders. It would be very expensive for lenders to identify all potential borrowers, and for borrowers to identify all potential lenders.

(4) Once a lender finds a potential borrower, he/she has the problem of finding out whether the borrower is likely to repay his debts. Financial intermediaries, on the other hand, have regular information of the financial situation and credibility of their clients by following the movements on their accounts. This gives them superior information as compared with outsiders in evaluating the risk related to a certain client.

(5) Financial intermediaries reduce the transaction costs which would have to be paid if every lender and borrower himself writes an appropriate loan contract, or pays the brokerage commission for the transaction. Smaller transaction costs related to one large loan as compared with many small loans creates economies

of scale (lower unit costs at a larger scale of operation) into the lending business.

(6) Financial intermediaries can create maturity transformations between financial agreements. From a continuous inflow of small short-term deposits from various sources with varying interest rates, a bank can issue large longterm loans with a fixed interest rate.

(7) The expertise and education of the personnel in banks allows them to make better investment decisions as compared with small savers with less information. The investing of large sums of money may though create large losses in the case banks make unsuccessful investment decisions.

(8) If a bank has enough independent depositors and borrowers, the risks related to one client do not threaten the existence of the whole bank, which might happen in the case of a small financial unit.

Financial Market Instruments

The distinction between money and capital markets is made on the basis of the maturity of the securities traded at the market. In practice, specific market places do not exist for these two markets, and the instruments traded in both markets are sold by the same financial intermediaries.

Definition: The maturity of a debt instrument is the length of the time (term) to that instrument's expiration date.

Definition: Money market is a financial market in which only shortterm debt and equity instruments (maturity less than one year) are traded.

Capital market, on the other hand, is the market where longer-term debt and equity instruments (maturity over one year) are traded.

Definition: By an equity we mean a financial instrument, which gives the holder of the equity a specified ownership concerning the underlying matter. For example, shares of common stock of firms are equities. _

A List of Money Market Instruments

(1) Negotiable bank certificates of deposit (CD) is a debt instrument sold by banks to their debtors. A CD pays a fixed annual interest and pays back the principal value at the date of maturity.

(2) U.S. Treasury bill is a short term debt instrument issued by U.S. government in three-, six-, and twelve-month maturity. T-bills pay the face (principal) value at maturity and do not pay interest, but they effectively pay interest by initially selling at discount, that is, at a price lower than the face value. For this reason they are also called zero-coupon-rate bonds. Tbills are the most liquid asset at money market with a minimum possibility of default (probability of not getting the promised payment), because they are actively traded and issued by the state.

(3) Commercial paper is short-term debt instrument issued by large banks and well-known corporations, such as General Motors or AT&T.

(4) Banker's acceptance is a bank draft (a promise of payment similar to a check) issued by a firm, payable at some future date and guaranteed for by a fee by the bank who stamps it as "accepted". The firm issuing the instrument is required to deposit the necessary funds into its account to cover the draft. If the firm fails to do so, the bank's guarantee obligate the bank to cover the draft. These "accepted" drafts are often resold in a secondary market (see the next section) at discount similarly as T-bills.

(5) Repurchase agreement (RP) is a short-term loan (usually with a maturity of less than two weeks) in which T-bills serve as collateral.

(6) Eurodollars are U.S. dollars deposited in foreign banks outside the United States or in the branches of U.S. banks in foreign countries.

(7) Federal funds are typically overnight loans between banks taken from their deposits at the Federal Reserve (the central bank of U.S.). This market is very sensitive to the credit needs of the banks so that the interest rate on these loans, called the federal funds rate, is a closely watched barometer of the tightness of the credit market.

A List of Capital Market Instruments

(1) Stocks are equity claims on the net income and assets of a corporation.

(2) Mortgages are loans given to individuals or business firms to purchase land, housing, or other real structures, where the structure or land serves as a collateral for the loan.

(3) Corporate bonds are long-term bonds issued by corporations with strong credit ratings. A typical corporate bond sends the holder an interest payment once or twice a year and pays back the face (nominal) value at maturity.

(4) U.S. Government securities are long-term debt instruments issued by the U.S. Treasury to finance the deficits of the federal government.

(5) U.S. Government Agency Securities are long-term bonds issued by government agencies usually guaranteed by the federal government.

(6) State and Local Government Bonds, also called municipal bonds, are long-term debt instruments issued by state and local governments to finance their expenditures on schools, roads, etc.

(7) Consumer and Bank Commercial Loans are loans to consumers and firms principally made by banks.

Usually, no secondary market exists for these loans and so they are the least liquid of all capital market instruments.

Primary and Secondary Financial Markets

There are principally two ways a firm or an individual can raise funds from financial markets. The most common method is to issue a debt instrument such as a bond or a mortgage.

Definition: A debt instrument is of short term if its maturity is a year or less, and is of long term if ten years or more. Debt instruments with a maturity between one and ten years are of intermediate term.

Another way to raise funds from a financial market is to issue equities, such as common stock, which are claims on the net income (income after expenses and taxes) and assets of the issuer (usually a business firm). If you own one share of the common stock of a company that has issued one million shares, you are entitled (have a claim) to one-millionth of the firm's future net income and assets. Equities usually make periodic payments called dividends to their shareholders, and are long-term securities because of not having a maturity date.

The main disadvantage of owning a corporation's equities rather than its debt instruments is that the equity holder is a residual claimant, that is, the corporation must pay its obligations to all its debt holders before it pays to its equity holders. On the other hand, the advantage of holding equities is that equity holders benefit directly from any increases in the corporation's profitability and/or asset value, since equities confer ownership rights to the equity holders. Debt holders will not benefit from the firm's increased profitability because the dollar payments of loans are fixed. However, the risks of holding equities are much greater than of holding debt instruments a firm has issued. These questions will be studied later in chapter.

Definition: A primary market is a financial market in which new issues of a security, such as a bond or a stock, are first time sold to initial buyers by the issuer, a corporation or a government agency.

Definition: A secondary market is a financial market in which securities that have been previously issued (and are thus of secondhand) can be resold.

Primary markets for securities are not well known to the public because the issuing of new securities takes place behind closed doors. The New York and American Stock Exchanges as well as Helsinki Stock Exchanges, on the other hand, are examples of secondary markets. Other examples of secondary markets are foreign exchange markets, futures markets and options markets. When an individual buys a security in a secondary market, the person who sells the security receives money in exchange for the security.

However, the corporation that has issued the security acquires no funds. A corporation acquires funds only when it issues new securities at the primary market.

Secondary markets serve for three functions. First, they allow the reselling of financial instruments in order to raise cash, which improves the liquidity of these instruments. The increased liquidity of financial instruments makes them more desirable, which helps the issuing firm to sell new securities at the primary market. Second, the higher the price of a certain security at the secondary market, the higher price the issuing firm can sell its corresponding new securities at the primary market, and thus the greater amount of money it can raise.

This connection between asset pricing at secondary and primary markets has focused the research on asset price behavior to be concentrated at secondary and not at primary markets. Third, secondary market opens a market to handle risk. Those who consider the instruments they hold too risky for them can sell these assets at the secondary market, and vice versa. This third function of secondary markets opens a possibility to share the risk of one economic unit between other units who are willing to cover a part of the risk at a proper price. The operation of insurance companies, for example, is completely based on this function.

Exchanges and Over-The-Counter Markets

Secondary markets can be organized basically in two ways: one way is to organize exchanges where the buyers and sellers of securities (or their agents called brokers) meet in one central location to conduct these trades. The New York and American Stock Exchanges as well as Helsinki Stock Exchanges for stocks and the Chicago Board of Trade for commodities (wheat, corn, silver, etc.) are examples of organized exchanges.

The other method to organize a secondary market is to have an Over-The-Counter (OTC)-market, in which dealers at different locations with inventories of securities buy and sell securities "over-the-counter" to anyone who is willing to accept their prices. Because the over-the-counter dealers are in computer contact with each other, and they know the prices set by each of them, the OTC market is very competitive and does not much differ from a market with organized exchange.

5

Endogenous Money and Banking Activity

This chapter attempts to highlight some key elements of the workings of modern banking. These elements are worth bearing in mind when constructing a monetary theory of production for an analytical explanation of banking activity based on the book-entry nature of money. Considering the endogenous-money view put forth by the Post-Keynesian tradition, the paper tries to show the importance of drawing a rigorous distinction between monetary and financial intermediation. It will point out the peculiar characteristics of monetary flows, discarding the approach in physical terms adhered to by both Post-Keynesians and circuit theorists. The analysis is illustrated by a stylised example of interbank clearing, which emphasises the logical distinction existing between money, credit, and deposits.

INTRODUCTION

> *'Banks do two things in this economy. First, they act as financial intermediaries. [...] Second, they provide transactions services, making payments as demanded by the households.' Stanley Fischer (1983: 4)*

> *'Until we get our concepts semantically in order, little progress in the dialogue and discussion over the cause vs effect role of money can be expected.' Paul Davidson (1988: 163)*

Over the past twenty years or so, a Post-Keynesian (PK hereafter) macroeconomic theory of monetary economies has been worked out, mainly in the United Kingdom and the United States (with ramifications in both continental Europe and Canada), whose origin may be traced back to the years of the Radcliffe Committee report.2 This theory aims at studying the workings of a monetised production economy in Keynes's sense, i.e. an entrepreneurial economic system where (bank) money is essential both in the short- and in the long-run. From the pioneering work of Kaldor (1970, 1986 [1982]), P. Davidson (1978 [1972]), P. Davidson and S. Weintraub (1973), S. Weintraub (1978), Kaldor and Trevithick (1981), and Minsky (1982)--to list only some of the most cited sources--, PK monetary theory has been developed and refined, with some analytical disagreement yet to be settled, by authors such as Moore (1979, 1983, 1985, 1988b, 1989b, 1991), Chick (1984, 1986, 1993, 1996), Lavoie (1984, 1985, 1992), Dow and Dow (1989), Rousseas (1989), Wray (1990, 1992, 1995), Palley (1991, 1996), Pollin (1991), Howells (1995, 1996), Arestis and Howells (1996), Dow (1996a, 1996b, 1997), and Arestis (1997).3 Without attempting here either a critical survey of this school of thought or an exegesis of Keynes's work,4 the hallmark of the PK research programme in monetary economics may be defined as twofold. It stems from the view that 'money matters', and elaborates on the idea that the supply of (bank) money is 'credit-driven and demand-determined'--to use two common PK expressions to which we shall return. To be sure, 'both phrases signify that money-holding, monetary exchange, money prices, monetary calculation, and the monetary financing of production are integral to a capitalist economy' (Cottrell 1994: 590).

It is no exaggeration to maintain that there is a general consensus among PK monetary theorists that money is the consequence of economic activity and not the cause of it. This view has been labelled the endogenous-money approach to modern production economies, in contrast with the exogenous monetary mass characterising monetarist theory and, more generally, neoclassical economics. However, there still exists a conceptual controversy as to what monetary endogeneity exactly means in the real world (see e.g. Davidson (1988: 156-63)).

On the one hand, the very notion of endogeneity may have different meanings, according to the focus of the analysis, and it is necessary to distinguish causality from controllability of economic variables (see e.g. Desai (1987), Moore (1988b: 144-64), and Wray (1992: 297-300)). On the other hand, there are points of disagreement on the structural relationship between monetary authority's policy reaction function and banks' behaviour (see e.g. Palley (1991, 1996), and Pollin (1991)). Central bank's intervention and interest rate policy are indeed the main focus of present competing views within this tradition, involving issues such as mark-up pricing policy and liquidity preference, both from the standpoint of the banking firm (see Hewitson (1995: 290-8) for a good overview).

This paper attempts to highlight some key elements of the workings of modern banking, which might be worth considering in order to construct a monetary theory of production providing an analytical explanation of banking activity in accordance with the (endogenous) nature of bank money. Within PK literature, the turning point of our approach has best been expressed by Moore, when he observed that '[p]erhaps the easiest way to understand the meaning of monetary endogeneity is to focus on the behavior of the banking system and the deposit creation process. As is well known, banks create transactions deposits whenever they grant loans. Banks are also financial intermediaries, and make a profit by lending at a markup over their borrowing rate' (Moore 1989a: 479, italics ours).

The point is worth emphasising, for it is often misunderstood--not to say entirely neglected--even by contemporary (PK) writers. Thus, Section 1 will present the analysis of financial intermediation from a 'bank money' point of view, along the broad lines of what probably is the most realistic theory of modern banking within a monetary production economy. Yet, authors like Kaldor and Moore (but many other Post-Keynesians as well) do not make (explicit) the crucial distinction between money and credit, so important for constructing a monetary theory of production in compliance with the banking nature of money. Furthermore, PK analysis does not distinguish money from bank deposits, since it is based on the idea that bank liabilities are money.

Section 2 focuses on these crucial issues. It will explore the primary function of monetary intermediation by referring to the work of Schmitt (1966, 1972, 1975, 1984), Cencini (1984, 1988, 1995, 1997, 1999) and, subsidiarily, of some adherents to the so-called theory of the monetary circuit (see Graziani (1988a, 1988b, 1990, 1994) for excellent surveys). Section 3 illustrates with a stylised example how important it is to be clear about the twofold nature of bank intermediation, by analysing the book-entry operations recorded for the settlement of interbank debt within a national economy. The last section provides some concluding remarks.

Banks as Financial Intermediaries

A common statement in PK monetary analysis has it that '[b]anks, after all, are essentially in the business of selling credit' (Moore 1988a: 373).8 To be precise, commercial banks participate in the process of financial intermediation, by means of which deficit-spending units borrow from saving units--via some middleman institutions for reasons that do not concern us here9--the proceeds they need to finance their net flow of expenditures. 'The banking system is an intermediary in the sense that it facilitates the transfer of real resources from surplus to deficit spending units' (Ball 1964: 168). As pointed out by Moore, '[l]ike all financial intermediaries, commercial banks make their profits on the rate spread between the asset and liability side of their balance sheets' (Moore 1988b: 49). Indeed, Moore is perhaps the author who has most emphasised the workings of the banking firm within the PK paradigm.11 According to him, '[b]anks may be considered as two-input, two-output firms. The two inputs (bank liabilities) are retail and wholesale deposits; the two outputs (bank assets) are retail and wholesale lending' (Moore 1985: 13).

Owing to the principle of double-entry accounting, total bank lending is identical to total bank deposits at any point of time for any individual bank and for the banking system as a whole, as we are going to see. In Tobin's words, 'depositors entrust to bankers whatever amounts the bankers lend' (Tobin 1987 [1963]: 272), since each and every loan is recorded--in one and the same act--on both sides of the bankers' balance sheet systematically. In fact, as suggested by Fama in his famous Journal of Monetary Economics paper, 'the concern with banks in macroeconomics centers on their role as portfolio managers, whereby they purchase securities from individuals and firms (and a loan is, after all, just a purchase of securities) which they then offer as portfolio holdings (deposits) to other individuals and firms' (Fama 1980: 44).

On that account, an important development of PK thought has centred on Keynes's (1936) liquidity preference theory, and more specifically on financial institutions' liquidity preference (see e.g. Dow (1996a: 498-504; 1997: 70-6)). Dow and Dow argue persuasively that, '[j]ust like non-bank wealth-holders, banks too are subject to liquidity preference in structuring their portfolios' (Dow and Dow 1989: 154). Since they operate in a non-ergodic economic system--where the future is uncertain and unpredictable (Davidson 1978 [1972])--, banks usually risk-assess the creditworthiness of their potential borrowers before passing any new loan agreement, a practice implemented by all financial institutions to avert collapse.

Now, what fundamentally distinguishes banks from other financial intermediaries--such as building societies in the United Kingdom or savings and loan funds in the United States--is the observation that only banks can 'create' means of payment (Tobin 1987 [1963]: 275). As noted by Wray, any economic agent can of course issue IOUs by acknowledging his or her debt towards another agent, 'but these [IOUs] cannot become "credit" or "money" unless they are accepted' (Wray 1995: 274).

The 'moneyness' of a (private) liability is portrayed as depending on the willingness of the public to accept it as a means of payment within a given geographic area. In other words, people use (bank) money because, so the argument goes, they all agree(d) to discharge their debts by means of it. This is indeed the convention-based analysis put forward by leading monetary practitioners (see Goodhart (1989 [1975]: 111)), and within the academic profession it is usually confirmed by the view that 'modern banking systems function on the bedrock of the confidence generated by the lender-of-last resort function of the central bank' (Dow 1996a: 498). All this will be elaborated in the following sections. Let us concentrate here on the canonical distinction between banks and other financial intermediaries.

Specifically, PK monetary theorists claim that 'it is possible for banks to advance credit to cover spending and then to recapture deposits' (Wray 1990: 267, italics ours). Indeed, as the argument goes, any bank experiencing a lack of deposits may always turn to the domestic central bank, to borrow the liquidity which ultimately guarantees the smooth functioning of the overall payment system. This exclusive property of the banking system is meant to correspond to the well-known principle according to which loans make deposits--the distinguishing tenet of unorthodox monetary theory (see e.g. Realfonzo (1998: Chapter 6))--, and contrasts with the traditional view that bank borrowing is the cause of bank lending ('deposits make loans'), as for any other (non-bank) financial institution. In the words of Kaldor and Trevithick, '[i]n a system where the money supply consists largely of deposits of private banks, an increase in bank lending is necessarily reflected in a corresponding increase in bank deposits, since the increased spending automatically swells the deposits of the recipients' (Kaldor and Trevithick 1981: 7).

Within this framework, reference to bookkeeping rules provides no analytical insight. Indeed the two-sidedness of banks' balance sheets is a battology for the analysis of the banking firm. An investigation focusing on either total accounting magnitudes or their dynamic variation over a given period of time cannot provide a satisfactory explanation of why loans make deposits. As a matter of fact, neither a static nor a dynamic analysis of banks' balance sheet can logically determine the direction of causality between loans and deposits, which are merely the two faces of the same reality: the existing money-income.

Attention must be paid to the final cause of bank lending in the process by means of which deposits are formed. In so doing, the 'income generating-finance process'--to use Davidson's (1988) phrase--must be considered, if we aim at constructing a monetary theory of production explaining why banking activity and the production process participate together in the same macroeconomic reality.17 As Lavoie puts it, '[a]ny production in a modern or in an "entrepreneur" economy is of a monetary nature' (Lavoie 1984: 774). Hence let us start from the allegation that '[t]he additional debts of banks are issued and used to accept and pay for additional offer contracts of producers and workers' (Davidson 1988: 164). For the sake of clarity, let us make tabula rasa of any existing bank deposit, so that the new flow of production must be financed entirely ex nihilo (to avoid the temptation to explain a deposit's formation by having recourse to a pre-existent deposit, whose origin would remain mysterious). In period P, firm F organises production following its 'animal spirits' and according to Keynes's (1936) principle of effective demand, and asks a bank, B, to pay the factors of this production: the wage-earners, W.

In the situation just described, PK monetary economists correctly emphasise that firms need to finance their expenditures on the factors market by obtaining the necessary loans from the banks. They are also right in noting that '[t]hese flows of credit then reappear as deposits on the liability side of the balance sheet of banks when firms use these loans to remunerate their factors of production' (Lavoie 1984: 774).19 All this verifies the causality from loans to deposits, and may substantiate the claim that 'the basic function of the banking system is to create new monetary units that make production (and, to a lesser extent, consumption) possible' (p. 775). What may still deserve investigating is the widespread belief that the banking system creates the necessary credit to finance the income-generating process (that is, current production).

Indeed, one must bear in mind Keynes's General Theory analysis, particularly where the author--after an entire chapter devoted to "The Choice of Units"--considers labour as literally the sole factor of production (Keynes 1936: 213-15). Granting the etymological definition of the word 'factor' (i.e. creator), one may ask if the banking system can logically create something of its own, in addition to the result of human effort. The answer is negative, at least at this stage of the analysis. On reflection, one may in fact observe that the credit granted by banks to firms to finance production has its ultimate origin in the credit granted by workers to banks, at the very moment current wages are paid. So much so that, ultimately, Hicks's distinction between an 'overdraft economy' and an 'autoeconomy' does not capture the essence of modern banking.

As a result of the payment of wages, F is necessarily debited by the bank with the cost of production, and its debt is entered on the assets side of the bank's balance sheet.

Indeed, this entry is recorded even if the firm were to finance production out of its cash flow, instead of using an overdraft facility provided by banks (through negotiation). Simultaneously, the factors of production own a positive purchasing power over current output in the form of a bank deposit, recorded as a liability for B. In the words of Graziani, '[a] picture of the economy taken immediately after the payment of wages would reveal that the whole of the existing money stock is a debt of the firms and a credit of wage earners towards the banks' (Graziani 1996: 143). Put differently, and as astonishing as it may appear, every production brings about the deposits necessary to finance it,22 independently of the behaviour of economic units (i.e. households and firms, inclusive of the general government sector).

The financing of production with a pre-existent deposit does not pertain to the anatomy of modern banking, and indeed cannot be explained in this context without implying metaphysical creations. Neither commercial banks, nor the banking system as a whole creates credit, as is still (too) often maintained within academic circles by referring to the anachronistic idea of seigniorage. In fact, this critique is but a restatement of the argument that, for banks, the only source of profits lies in an efficient portfolio management by means of which their interest rates' spread is maximised. In other words, banks do not create income by themselves when they monetise the production process through the payment of wages. Their role, though essential for the macroeconomy, has nothing to do with the 'spontaneous generation' of purchasing power, which must be produced in order to exist in reality. As noticed by Fama, 'the payments mechanism provided by banks is a pure accounting system of exchange wherein transfers of wealth take place via debits and credits that give rise to sales and purchases of securities in the portfolios against which the sending and receiving accounts have claims' (Fama 1980: 47).

On the whole; it is possible to claim that the volume of bank lending both determines and is at once determined by bank borrowing.23 To the extent that the principle of effective demand enables firms to determine their needs for 'initial finance',24 bank loans to remunerate the factors of current output lead to the simultaneous formation of equivalent deposits to the benefit of workers. Because of the two-sidedness of banks' balance sheet, reinterpretation of this operation shows in the last analysis that the newly-formed deposits are lent ipso facto to firms, to cover current production costs by means of the financial market. Wage-earners save in fact all their current income at the very moment firms pay their remuneration. So much so that workers thus own a financial capital which they will spend later to obtain in real terms what they already own under the monetary form of bank deposits (Schmitt 1984: 484-92). 'The reality of our modern monetary systems is thus based on the simultaneous application of the two principles, "loans make deposits" and "deposits make loans", where the first refers to the fact that deposits are created through the loans granted by banks to firms, while the second states that the deposits earned by workers are immediately lent to firms to cover financially their costs of production' (Cencini 1997: 275).

Thus some clarifications are in order, before further investigating the workings of modern payment systems. At this stage, the reader might indeed point to the pretended circularity of the above explanation, so that the whole argument of this paper would be fatally flawed, and therefore easily dismissed. Are we claiming that loans make deposits which make loans, in an infinite (time-dimensional) causal chain that ultimately may be interpreted as a multiplication of the original magnitude? Are we claiming that wage-earners must willingly lend the newly-formed deposits to firms as soon as the latter remunerate the 'productive services' of the former, in order to avoid fatal 'leakages' that may spark off an economic crisis? Are we claiming that firms can always obtain on the market for produced goods the 'final finance' they need to repay their debts towards the rest of the economy? Are we claiming that banks always accommodate any loan request by entrepreneurs in search of the initial finance necessary to implement new production plans? The answers to these questions are all negative. Let us try to substantiate them briefly by taking the relevant questions in the reverse order.

As argued by PK structuralists, commercial banks may, and indeed do, vary the interest rate charged for new loans, according to the assessment of the risk involved in opening new credit lines. The amount of credit granted by banks to firms is in fact influenced by perceived borrowers' risk, and varies with respect to borrowers' creditworthiness, the causal factor being the specific rate of interest fixed by the lending institution on a case-by-case basis (see e.g. Dow (1997: 74-5)). An argument put forward by the liquidity preference school within PK monetary theory concerns indeed banks' behaviour in case of an economic downturn, when some projects do not raise the necessary funds because of pessimistic expectations generated within a non-ergodic system.

Yet simple accounting logic reveals that, once granted, every bank loan brings about the simultaneous formation of identical deposits within the domestic banking system. In Chick's words, '[t]hese deposits must be held somewhere in the economy, willingly or unwillingly, and the increased holdings count as saving, voluntary or involuntary' (Chick 1996: 13-14). No leakage is logically possible. The essential mechanic rule of double-entry bookkeeping averts it. To fear a leakage from the banking system in the process of financial intermediation is a contradiction in terms, even when international speculation is brought into the picture.

Yet the fact that bank deposits cannot leave the (banking) system until they are destroyed by firms' repayment of the corresponding debts, does not mean that firms can always sell all their current output on the market for produced goods. In short, as PK writers have stressed correctly, 'animal spirits' may turn out to be wrong, and consequently some items might be unsold on the goods market.

However, to focus on the points at issue here, if we concentrate attention on deposit formation only, we understand (as it may be inferred from above) that firms' unsold goods and services on the corresponding markets are necessarily sold on the financial market, when wage-earners automatically lend to firms the newly-formed deposits (i.e. current income) via banks' intermediation.

As soon as income is born, it is thus lent by its holders until its "withdrawal". This means that income is instantaneously transformed into saving or, identically, into capital' (Schmitt 1984: 158, our translation). As a matter of fact, it must be recalled that until final purchase on the goods market takes place--where consumption occurs in strictly economic terms--, workers (or more generally income holders) own a claim over a bank deposit that testifies their financial ownership over the newly-produced output. In a nutshell, as soon as wages are paid, wage-earners (willingly or not) substitute their bank deposits with a drawing right over current output, so much so that the corresponding deposits are lent at once to firms, in an operation testifying the latter's debt resulting from production. This 'mechanical' lending means--let us say it once more--that when they remunerate the production factors, firms automatically borrow all the newly-formed income (enabling them to finance current production) from (and independently of the behaviour of) original income holders, W.

To summarise, the working of modern banking is essentially unaffected by agents' forms of behaviour, once bank managers have decided to grant a loan to finance production (on the basis of a creditworthiness assessment that might of course take into account the bank's liquidity preference schedule). As a matter of fact, for any bank the unorthodox linkage that runs from making loans to collecting deposits must be understood within the mechanics of double-entry accounting recording payments on the factors market. Simple economic analysis of the bookkeeping entry resulting from the income generating-finance process makes it also clear that the ultimate financing of production cannot be created by the banking system, which intervenes as a mere catalyst.

Infinite recursive causality between loans and deposits is broken down by understanding that any bank deposit is originally formed on the labour market as the result of firms' borrowing to remunerate production factors, and the ultimate source of bank financing of production lies in the wage-earners' simultaneous deposit formation. Further, deposit multiplication is ruled out as soon as one perceives that payments on the goods market are of the opposite algebraic sign to payments on the factors market. Clearly, a deposit's formation on the latter is the first leg of a macroeconomic phenomenon that has the same deposit's destruction on the former as its second leg, the two legs being logically separated in chronological time.

BANKS AS MONETARY INTERMEDIARIES

As the previous section has shown, deposit formation is the result of the 'joint effort' of banking and the production process. More precisely, banks emit a number of money units for the remuneration of current workers, whose product is the very content of the newly-formed deposits. In other words, the banking system issues the monetary form where matter and energy are moulded into according to the project devised by human beings and implemented within the productive sphere. 'From the beginning, banking and productive systems thus contribute to the determination of a unique macroeconomic structure' (Cencini 1997: 276).

In neoclassical terms, the monetary sector and the real sector operate concomitantly to determine the macroeconomic magnitude par excellence: money-income. In PK terms, monetary endogeneity is best explained by the relation established between bank lending and entrepreneurs' 'animal spirits' every time the expected effective demand is deemed profitable for the banking firm as well. The payment of wages is the operation that gives rise to a (newly-formed) bank deposit, a drawing right over current output in the hand of wage-earners or, generally speaking, of all economic units who take their place as income holders. So, as Lavoie (1984: 774-5) observed, the income generating-finance process ends up forming a money stock.

Yet it is worth stressing at this juncture that the money stock never is a sum of money proper. In fact, the result of bank lending is a certain amount of bank deposits, the sum of the latter defining the existing monetary stock.31 But as Arestis and Howells have recently emphasised in their "Theoretical Reflections on Endogenous Money", there remains a problem in trying to capture the essentials of the flow of bank lending in an analysis concentrating on the behaviour of the money stock. As Arestis has it, '[there] is a logical objection to trying to represent an analysis of flows in a diagram designed to show the behaviour of stocks' (Arestis 1997: 56). Specifically, Arestis and Howells suggest going beyond the tradition of drawing money supply curves--that is, using stock diagrams--, by investigating the realised flow 'resulting from the interaction of the demand for credit with the demand for the resulting deposits' (Arestis and Howells 1996: 550).

Like the great majority of professional economists, however, Arestis and Howells make use of a conception of economic flows strongly influenced by physics. The realised flow resulting from the interaction quoted above is in fact a stock 'on the wing' (to use Robertson's language). Like the motion of a mobile in a given space (over a set time span, which enables one to measure velocity), the monetary flow-

-or the flow of money--is indeed assimilated by Arestis and Howells (but by many others, too) to an observable movement of the corresponding-stock, i.e. a deposit circulation from lenders (say, W) to borrowers (F, in the case of the financing of production) through the banking system's balance-sheet identity.

Now, quite apart from the simultaneity of loans and deposits in the income generating-finance process investigated above, in monetary economics the idea of a flow being a stock set into motion--at a given (or variable) velocity, as in the physical world--might be questioned analytically. As a matter of fact, in his synthesis of the so-called circuit theory relating money and production, Lavoie maintains that '[i]nitially, money appears under the form of a flow. It is only at the end of the circuit that money will become a stock' (Lavoie 1987: 71-2, our translation). This means that money is a flow, whose result is a stock under the form of a bank deposit. Unlike, say, water, oil or blood, money is not a (liquid) stock that can flow in a pre-existent circuit. Whilst any hydraulic circuit, or pipeline, exists independently of the 'matter' flowing into it, the circuit of money does not exist (cannot be retraced) independently of money. According to the modern theory of the monetary circuit, there is thus a strong case for breaking down the link with physics, and to start thinking in different (macroeconomic) terms. We shall explore this route in the remainder of this section.

As Bernard Schmitt put it in personal conversation recently (May 1996), 'double-entry accounting records the result of monetary flows and not the flows themselves'. In-depth analysis of monetary endogeneity should therefore start from a bookkeeping attempt to depict the very flows giving rise to the money stock.

Banks cannot create anything, the only possible net creation resulting from the intellectual effort of human beings who project a more useful form matter and energy may be moulded into. All that banks can do is to start from zero and maintain the statu quo, as their balance-sheet identity easily demonstrates at any point in time. Yet the very process of bank intermediation enables banks to create simultaneously a positive number of money units (x) and the same negative number of money units (x), in any payment they issue for the public. Starting from zero (0) banks can in fact create the pair { x ; x}, whose elements add up to zero indeed (x x 0), but that also entails the creation of a positive and a negative number (x) 'counting' the payment at hand objectively.

To refer to the income generating-finance process, '[t]he definition of a negative sum of money is quite precise: even in the case where the firm owns a sufficient amount of "circulating capital", the bank pays the factor of production, [W], by debiting the enterprise. With respect to the bank, [W] holds a net credit (i.e. a positive sum of money) and, correspondingly, the firm holds a net debit (a negative sum of money)'. It is thus possible to substantiate the argument put forth, where we maintained that no payment on the factors market is (or can be) financed with prior saving logically. The same argument applies in fact to any other payment, on the goods market and on financial markets as well, in so far as the payer is debited by the bank issuing the payment even if (s)he owns a pre-existent (positive) deposit.

Let us briefly investigate a payment on the financial market, where an already-existing deposit is transferred from its initial holder, IH, to a borrower. Suppose indeed that client C asks his bank for a 'consumption loan'. If C can satisfy the bank's managers with the necessary guarantees of repayment at the due date, the loan is granted (at the negotiated interest rate). In bookkeeping terms, the result is entered as (2) (where y < x).

The first entry (1) in Table 2 records the result of the current income generating-finance process, inasmuch as firms are indebted towards the banking system for the newly-formed deposits (on the simplifying assumption that they do not have a wage-fund at their disposal to compensate their current debt with a pre-existent credit). The second entry (2) is the result of bank intermediation as requested by one of its clients, C, who borrows a part (y) of the income owned by IH. Entry (3) simply is the net outcome of the two previous entries, and demonstrates that IH and C have, together, the purchasing power necessary to consume total current output, that is, the very object of F's debt.

Now, it might be useful to observe that the monetary flows giving rise to entry (2) are the sine qua non condition for the exchange between C and IH on the financial market. Let us consider both the monetary aspect and the financial aspect of the relevant bank intermediation in a single picture.

To concentrate attention on monetary flows first, one may observe that y units of money are created positively and negatively for both agents, C and IH, in one and the same motion (i.e. an electric impulse). In bookkeeping terms, C is credited-debited with y units of money (flows 1 and 2), as is the case for IH (flows 3 and 4) simultaneously. The purpose of this monetary intermediation is precisely to enable C to borrow the requested income from IH. It is testified by C's cession of non-bank financial claims (e.g. securities) in exchange for a claim over a bank deposit previously held by IH. Bank financial intermediation is indeed the transfer of current purchasing power from present income holders to borrowers, in exchange for the right given to lenders, IH, to withdraw in the future an equivalent deposit (inclusive of interest capitalisation) originally owned by C. As the late Sir John Hicks vividly noted in his posthumous Market Theory of Money:

> The purchaser of a bill is, in effect, making a loan to the issuer; he is willing to lend, in this form, because he is assured [...] that the loan, when the time comes, will be repaid. [...] The lender has just to wait until the "ship comes

home". Even before that happens, the bill is represented by the cargo, or some part of it, so that the lender can think of himself as entitled to something more than a promise; indeed, as we saw, he has something against which he can exercise a legal claim. (Hicks 1989: 52)

To sum up, one can observe that payments on the factors market as well as on the financial market are carried out through the circular flow of money, leaving behind a series of bookkeeping entries that define the result of, respectively, the formation and the transfer of money-income. It should take only a moment's reflection to convince the reader that payments on the goods market are issued according to the same principle, firms taking the place of income holders in an operation that represents the consumption of current output in economic terms, that is, the destruction of money-income (see Schmitt (1984: 405-27) and Cencini (1988: 82-97; 1995: 15-21) for further developments).

The conclusion of this line of argument is that monetary and financial intermediation are the two faces of every payment, and can be understood only by a rigorous investigation of the book-entry nature of money. Within any national economy, bank money is endogenously issued as the numerical means of payment every time an economic transaction takes place, the object of the latter being output under the form of a bank deposit. As we have been trying to show, income is formed (on the factors market), transferred (on financial markets), and destroyed (on the goods market) via bank intermediation in its double function of 'money-purveying' and 'credit-purveying'--to use Keynes's words.

It is thus possible to observe, ultimately, that every payment is analogous to the emission of a quantum of light, in the sense that it has both a wave-like characteristic and a corpuscular characteristic. The wave-like emission is the monetary flow of positive and negative numbers; the 'particle' is the associated real flow of output under the form of bank deposits, which are thus a store of value in the ultimate analysis. To quote Vallageas, '[t]he object of the circuit cannot be anything else than the value of the real object, because money does not exist indeed: it is but a form of the real object, called commodity' (Vallageas 1985: 51, our translation).

An Example of Bank (dual) Intermediation: the Clearing System

So far, to simplify discussion we have assumed a monetary production economy with a single bank, B, that could also be considered analytically as the banking system as a whole. To provide further analytical evidence in support of the argument we have been developing, it is time to introduce the two tiers of the banking system explicitly. In fact, modern payment systems involve a multitude of banks within any developed economy, and often a transaction implies the intervention of more than a single bank for the payment to be made. This raises the question of how any bank, B1, can make a payment in favour of another bank, B2, within the same monetary system.

Assume, for example, that the above-analysed operation on the factors market, between a firm and its workers, involves Barclays Bank and Lloyds Bank as, respectively, the bank of the payer (F) and the bank of one of the payees (W).

As is well known among both practitioners and experts of banking systems, '[t]he banks do not accept bank money in interbank transactions, but ultimately require their claims to be settled in central bank money' (Deutsche Bundesbank 1994: 46). Indeed, as is the case with the public, no bank whatsoever can make a payment on its own simply by issuing its spontaneous acknowledgement of debt towards any other bank within the national economy. In so far as every payment concerning the (non-bank) public must be issued by a third party (i.e. a bank), as the examples of the previous sections have shown, each transaction in the interbank market--that is, the market where commercial banks settle their reciprocal debts--has to be literally monetised by the intervention of an institution super partes. As Graziani neatly puts it, '[t]he role of the Central Bank is in fact of acting as third party between single banks so far as their reciprocal payments are concerned' (Graziani 1990: 18).

This is tantamount to saying that the essence of central banking is to catalyse interbank payments, the central bank acting as the bank of the various commercial banks operating in a pyramidal system where the latter deal with the public (i.e. firms and households, whereas the general government sector usually banks directly with the central bank).

Let us suppose, to simplify, that the payment recorded is the unique transaction over the period (say, a business day) considered for the settlement of interbank imbalances. The central bank has to intervene in order to clear the reciprocal positions of Barclays and Lloyds, so that the latter can really be paid for its transaction with the former by the end of the day.

As a central bank official has it, 'the Bank of England operates the core of the payment system, effecting the transfers between the banks which are direct members of the system' (Trundle 1998: 1). By holding settlement accounts for all banks participating in CHAPS,51 the Bank of England plays indeed the role of monetary intermediary between Barclays and Lloyds, taking over both the debt and the credit formed in the 'horizontal' interbank market, and substituting them with two corresponding 'vertical' relations.

Now, if the clearing operation ended up, the central bank would issue its spontaneous acknowledgement of debt in an operation that ultimately leaves the payee's bank (Lloyds) unpaid. In fact, at this stage of the payment, the positions in the interbank system are not settled yet. Lloyds

Bank has a credit towards the Bank of England, recorded in its settlement account in central bank money to replace an equivalent credit towards Barclays (the latter having a debt towards the central bank in replacement of the corresponding debt towards Lloyds). In practice, '[t]he Bank [of England] does not pay interest on balances held on these accounts' (European Monetary Institute 1996: 617) and the indebted bank must settle its position in central bank money by the end of the day (at the latest).

So, Lloyds spends its deposit at the Bank of England immediately, to purchase the financial assets that Barclays is selling in order to capture--either directly or through its cash account held by the clearing institution--the funds necessary to clear its position (that is, to repay its debt) towards the central bank. 'Whether these assets are deposited within the clearing house's accounts as "real securities" of the member banks, or supplied when final settlements are due, is irrelevant' (Cencini 1995: 41).

Considering the whole clearing operation, one can thus easily observe the neutrality of central bank intervention in the interbank system. The settlement accounts at the Bank of England are cleared at the end of the CHAPS day--but possibly instantaneously, within real-time gross settlement (RTGS) systems--, in so far as both commercial banks are credited-debited (or debited-credited) in central bank money, for an interbank payment that ultimately enables them to transfer a purchasing power from one to the other.

As a matter of fact, the securities sold by Barclays to fund its imbalance towards Lloyds (or towards the central bank, after substitution) represent a financial claim over domestic output, deposited within the banking system. Specifically, the financial assets recorded in Lloyds' balance sheet represent the goods and services that are the object of F's debt towards Barclays. Hence they represent in the ultimate analysis W's property right over the fraction of current production that corresponds precisely to his/her remuneration. Indeed, F's debt recorded by Barclays Bank has the current output owned by W as its object (as would be the case with a single bank, the whole transaction being mediated by the two tiers of the interbank payment system.

Now, the preceding discussion may be referred to in order to invalidate the traditional analysis underlying the lender-of-last-resort (LLR) function of the central bank. As Moore observes, '[t]he terminology "lender of last resort" has come to be associated with lending to financial institutions that are in serious difficulty' (Moore 1988b: 119). In terms of 'critical realism', from this 'partial event-regularity' most (PK) studies in monetary economics have proceeded on the assumption that '[c]entral banks are the residual monopoly suppliers of domestic liquidity.

They are always able to buy unlimited quantities of assets for their portfolios. They finance these purchases simply by issuing their own liabilities, which are domestic money'. In the light of the distinction between monetary and financial intermediation, the confusion between the money-purveying and the credit-purveying function should be evident by now.

As a matter of fact, the clearing mechanism briefly investigated above makes it plain that interbank debts are settled in central bank money through a transfer of selected eligible assets between commercial banks.

Central bank intermediation only provides the (numerical) means of payment, the (real) object of it being non-bank financial assets (securities) that have nothing to do with any alleged monetary creation whatsoever. Let us reconsider our stylised example. In fact, the Bank of England does not buy the bonds sold by Barclays for its portfolio.

All in all, to focus on the issue central to this section, central bank intervention is not to be mixed up with the medieval idea of seigniorage, because no single unit of purchasing power is created in the whole clearing process. Money-income results from the monetisation of current production costs only, even when the payer's and the payee's banks are distinct as in the case at hand.

Since W is a client of a bank different from F's one, the latter has to recover--through liability management--the deposit originated by the credit granted to the firm. Until this has been done, in fact, the bank of the payee has a promise to pay only, an issue bound to raise the problem known as 'payment float' in the jargon of settlement systems' experts.

Owing to the vehicular nature of money, the spontaneous acknowledgement of debt issued by Barclays conveys the information that Lloyds is indeed going to be paid. In order to do so, Barclays must issue bank bonds or, more generally, has to sell financial assets on the interbank market, so as to borrow from its counterpart (either directly or, more probably, via central bank mediation so as to make it seem at first sight a loan of last resort) the newly-formed purchasing power necessary for the final settlement.

The disequilibrium in the interbank market is cleared daily--or immediately within RTGS systems--through the workings of the clearing process, where the LLR intervention of the central bank is, in theory and in practice as well, a mere intermediation (involving both a monetary and a financial aspect) within the national banking system.

CONCLUSION

A brief analysis of modern payment systems that distinguishes the twofold (and simultaneous) function of banks as monetary and financial intermediaries has been attempted here, along the lines of the endogenous-money debate. A monetary theory of production explaining the income generating-finance process through the distinction of monetary and financial intermediation may be an important step towards the understanding of the workings of book-entry payment systems.

So much so that nowadays the development of both electronic funds transfer systems and e-money products makes it perhaps more difficult to grasp the very nature of money by simply looking at banks' balance sheet composition (and expansion).

Further, considering the monetary circuit as the movement of the money stock among bank depositors does not go to the root of the phenomenon. The relevant theoretical analyses put forth by leading 'circulationists' (also dubbed circuitistes) do not go so far as to consider the asset-liability definition of bank money.

As Deleplace and Nell (1996: 12) point out in their "Introduction" to the Post-Keynesian and circulation approaches to money, the exact meaning of monetary endogeneity remains ambiguous in both schools of thought. The ambiguity is reinforced by a rather loose conceptual analysis of money and credit, the two being often conceived of as proxies for the same 'monetary object'. Yet, 'explaining the peculiarity of money, specifically how it differs from finance, is a necessary piece of any theory of a monetary economy' (Deleplace and Nell 1996: 33), which is precisely what this paper strives to clarify.

An in-depth investigation into the very process of (endogenous) money emission has perhaps its most useful implications for the analysis of actual macroeconomic pathologies such as inflation and unemployment.

By explaining the anatomy of monetary production economies, where the banking system intervenes as a pure intermediary between economic agents, the new monetary theory can ultimately highlight the origin of the peculiar discrepancies existing in a disorderly payment system. Starting from the mechanisms governing monetary order, and in particular from the vehicular nature of bank money, one can indeed explain why a given domestic economy suffers from an excessive demand that may have a depressing effect on money's purchasing power.

This 'structural' monetary analysis of a macroeconomic morbidity like inflation is based on an economic framework in which the (logical) distinction between money emission and financial intermediation is not yet conformed to empirically in present-day banking systems. The current endogeneity-of-money view and the related theory of banking activity fail to recognise this disorder, so that our notes on the workings of modern payment systems have to end here.

6

Central Bank as Clearing House

The Payments System provides the arteries or highways for conducting trade, commerce and other forms of economic activities in any country. An efficient payments system functions as a lubricant speeding up the liquidity flow in the economy and creating a momentum for economic growth. The payments process is a vital aspect of financial intermediation; it enables the creation and transfer of liquidity among different economic agents. A smooth, well functioning payments system not only ensures efficient utilisation of scarce resources but also eliminates systemic risks.

The payments system assumes importance in the context of domestic financial sector reforms and global financial integration. The time value of money flows has increased sharply in view of the competing demands on the financial sector. Efficient, low cost cross-border payments flow helps to promote international trade in goods and services. Foreign investments (direct and portfolio) are encouraged by the availability of an efficient payments system.

For these reasons, an efficient and technologically advanced payments and settlement system performs a vital infrastructural function in the economy. Central banks have, therefore, been taking measures to set up such an infrastructural set up.

Use of money for settlement of payment obligations has a very long history. Use of non-cash exchange through barter preceded the introduction of money. Barter, however, co-exists with monetised economy in some underdeveloped agricultural societies even now. But currency or cash, is the most readily accepted medium of exchange in all modern societies because it is the legal tender and helps to bring about irrevocable settlement.

There are, however, certain disadvantages associated with the use of cash. Holding cash does not fetch any return-the interest foregone because of cash holding is a cost to the holder of cash. Besides, the holder of cash bears some insurance costs in terms of the premia that is paid to cover any loss/theft. Moreover, carrying of large quantities of cash to make large-value payments is a security risk and also involves transportation costs.

The requirements of a modern economy in regard to settlement of transactions are diverse and variegated and the needs of manufacturing, trade, and commerce activities involve large value payments over vast geographic distances. External trade with the rest of the world involves payments in different currencies. Payments can no longer be completed by simple cash transfer in such cases. Therefore, there arises the need for additional forms of payments, which can be facilitated with improved financial intermediation and expansion of financial instruments. Cheques and other paper based instruments and to some extent electronic instruments have become important modes of payment in recent times in most countries because of growing financial intermediation.

Individuals, business entities or governments issue cheques or other forms of order on their banks in discharge of their payment obligations. The recipients of these orders would then get the funds embodied in these payment instruments through their own banks. As the number of banks grew over time, the volume of instruments exchanged among them increased substantially. Consequently, as also to have an orderly means of transfer of payment instructions among banks at a location or centre, a common set of practices and mechanisms of exchange had to be evolved.

When instruments presented by customers of banks become payable at outside locations, special collection arrangements are set in motion to collect the funds. If the collecting bank has a branch at the relevant outside location, there would be no problem, but, if the collecting bank does not have a branch at the outside location, it will have to enter into correspondent banking relationship with another bank at the said outside location for the purpose of collecting funds.

The payment instruments which are routed through financial intermediaries involve book entries at various levels to transfer funds from one party to the other. The range of intermediation varies to take care of different situations. This may, for instance, consist of instructions to intermediaries to move goods coinciding with the movement of funds as in the case of a Letter of Credit. Or, the instruction could be for payment of specified sums of money to the bearer of a payment instrument, as in the case of a bearer cheque. In some cases, the payment instruments are negotiable in the sense that they can be transferred from person to person in lieu of cash.

In yet other cases, both the ultimate beneficiary and the destination could be pre-determined. In all these cases, banks play a crucial part in conveying, transmitting and carrying out the instructions embodied in the payment instruments. While doing so, these intermediaries have to settle among themselves the monetary claims arising from the execution of payment instructions. Thus, whenever non-cash payment instruments are involved, they are accompanied by a chain of related fund transfers as well as a stream of book entries and messages. Banks in turn need an intermediate agency such as the clearing house where these instruments can be exchanged and where the financial claims on one another can be settled through a settlement bank, which is usually the Central Bank of the country.

Clearing Houses facilitate the exchange of instruments and processing of payment instructions at a central point among the participating banks. Clearing Houses-manual and paper based in many advanced countries have gradually extended their range of activities to include automated (ACH) and electronic means for settlement of payment transactions. Such an evolution is also seen in emerging economies.

Banks, as crucial intermediaries in the payments stream, provide deposit accounts to non bank agents (i.e. individuals, firms/corporate bodies) which are considered as liquid assets and facilitate payments transactions. Banks provide credit facilities so that such payments can be effected with lower working balances. Moreover, they act as conduit through which domestic and international capital markets provide resources to the commercial sector.

The payments system has a multiplicity of layers where several levels of intermediation occur in the transfer of funds from one person and/or institution to another. The structure of the Payments System can be visualised as a Pyramid, with linkages among different tiers of the payment intermediaries. At the base of the Pyramid are the non banks (all non-depository corporations including individuals and firms) whose assets are diverse, including bank notes and deposits. The types of payments at the base of the Pyramid include both cash and non-cash modes of payments. Banks are at the intermediate level.

The assets of the banks comprise, among others, their reserves with the Central Bank, deposits with the correspondents and claims on the correspondents, and investments in Government and other securities, loans and advances and cash in their vaults. Typically, their liabilities would among others, be made up of deposits from non banks and correspondents and loans from the Central Bank. The Clearing House and the settlement bank are the financial intermediaries who channel the funds flow between the banks. At the apex of the pyramid is the Central Bank of the country (i.e. Reserve Bank of India) which has the settlement accounts of the banks and sustains the payments process.

In the Payments System Pyramid, the Central Bank has a special role to play as the settling bank maintaining settlement accounts for banks. These are used by banks to discharge their obligations amongst themselves. While the settlement account can be maintained with any bank, there is always a risk of default by the settling bank. A failure of a settling bank can have disastrous consequences leading to a possible systemic collapse. Settlement accounts maintained with the Central Bank, on the other hand, provide the basic stability to the settlement process as the Central Banks cannot fail. The involvement of the Central Bank in the settlement process is therefore crucial.

This monograph is organised in the following way. After giving a brief account of the evolution of payments system in India in Chapter II, the various paper based instruments in vogue in India are discussed in Chapter III. The complexities of the existing paper based payments and settlement systems, Remittance Facilities and Currency Chests and the Uniform Regulations and Rules of Clearing for paper based instruments form the subject matter of Chapter IV. Given the increase in the volume of paper based instruments and the time taken for clearing these instruments, it was inevitable to move towards item-based computerised processing and settlement for improving systemic efficiency as well as customer service.

These and other related aspects are the main themes of interest in Chapter V. In the early and mid 90s, a beginning was made in introducing ACH (Automated Clearing House) services such as Electronic Clearing Service (ECS) and Electronic Funds Transfer (EFT). The developments in this regard, including the establishment of a Shared Payment Network System (SPNS) of Automated Teller Machines (ATMs) are highlighted in Chapter VI. For an efficient electronic payments system, a strong and robust telecommunication network is necessary. The efforts made by the Reserve Bank in particular as well as the banking industry in general in setting up a telecommunication network to serve the needs of the industry form the contents of Chapter VII. The final chapter provides a brief idea of the challenges ahead in modernising the Indian payments system.

INSTITUTIONAL ARRANGEMENTS

The payments process can be facilitated by evolving appropriate institutional arrangements. Cash payment is best facilitated, for example, by the Reserve Bank issuing bank notes at all its offices and by the Reserve Bank providing a currency chest (to store currency on its behalf) in the premises of the agent (commercial banks, Government treasuries, sub-treasuries) where the Reserve Bank offices do not exist. The currency chest helps to distribute currency all over the country. Other institutional arrangements include agencies like the clearing house, settlement accounts with a major bank or (more often) the Central Bank and a framework of rules and procedures that are accepted by all concerned.

Traditional arrangements involved the exchange of cheques, computation of net payment obligations among the participating banks and settlement of claims through funds transfers in the books of the settling bank. In some countries, notably, England, the number of banks participating in clearing, the clearing banks, are limited. Other banks would route their instruments through one of the clearing members. The place where the exchange of instruments occurs and the claims are settled is known as the Clearing House.

All payment instructions made through the medium of cheques are debit transactions. A debit transaction occurs when the intended recipient initiates the payment transaction by depositing the instrument in his bank. During the course of a business day a number of instruments are deposited with a bank for collection by its customers. These instruments may be drawn on different branches of various banks and a collecting bank has to physically present the instruments for collection to each drawee bank/branch. The clearing system provides a convenient and well established institutional mechanism to take care of the problem of physical delivery of instruments as well as funds transfer between different banks.

In India, the clearing system is local and confined to a defined jurisdiction covering all the banks and branches situated in the area under a particular zone. The clearing house is a voluntary association of banks under the management of a bank where the settlement accounts are maintained. Wherever Reserve Bank of India has its office (and a banking department), the clearing house is managed by it. In the absence of an office of the Reserve Bank, the clearing house is managed by the State Bank of India, its associate banks and in a few cases by public sector banks.

Clearing Houses in India: There are 860 Bankers clearing houses in India, of which 840 are managed by State Bank of India and its Associates, 14 by Reserve Bank of India, and the rest 6 by nationalised banks. Reserve Bank of India manages 14 clearing houses at Ahmedabad, Bangalore, Bhubaneshwar, Mumbai, Calcutta, Chennai, Guwahati, Hyderabad, Jaipur, Kanpur, Nagpur, New Delhi, Patna and Thiruvananthapuram. These cover most of the major urban and semi-urban centres of economic activity. Other than the major cities and metropolitan centres, the volume and value of cheques cleared are very low. The cheques cleared in the clearing houses managed by Reserve Bank of India account for 62% in terms of volume and 86% in terms of value of the total cheques cleared in the country.

State Bank of India (SBI) has the widest network of branches in the country and acts as an agent of the Reserve Bank in centres where the RBI does not have its offices. It is therefore, natural that a vast majority of the clearing houses in the country are managed by the SBI. The rest of the clearing houses are managed by the associate banks of the SBI in the areas of their concentration and in some cases by other public sector banks.

The membership of the clearing house includes both direct members and sub-members. All the branches of a member bank within the clearing house jurisdiction are eligible to present and receive cheques drawn on any other member bank/branch within the jurisdiction. The sub-members, who are sponsored by a member bank, participate in clearing in the same way as a branch of a member bank.

Clearing Structure: The dominant feature of the Indian Banking system is its branch-centered banking. The vast network of branches implies that the logistics of collection and delivery of paper payment instruments becomes formidable.

The Mumbai Bankers' Clearing House, for instance, has over 110 members, 261 sub-members and extends over 2400 branches. The clearing infrastructure is designed to address the movement of instruments between the presenting and drawee branches. Each member bank in a centre is represented in the clearing house by its service branch which collects all the instruments from various branches and consolidates them for presentation to all the banks in the clearing house. Similarly, it receives and distributes among its branches all the instruments drawn upon its branches by other banks in the clearing house. The service branch of a bank performs a crucial intermediary role between the clearing house and the branch of a bank.

Clearing Process: The clearing process begins with the deposit of a cheque in a bank. The cheque (along with other cheques) is delivered to the bank/branch where it is drawn. The cheque is passed for payment if the funds are available and the banker is satisfied about the genuineness of the instrument. The cheques that are unpaid are returned to the presenting bank through another clearing called the Return Clearing. The realisation of the funds occurs after the completion of return clearing and by the absence of an unpaid cheque.

Settlement of Funds: The settlement of funds in clearing occurs at several levels. The aggregate amount or value of cheques presented by a bank on other banks represents the claim by that bank on other banks. Similar claims are made by all the banks on every other bank in the clearing. A net settlement is arrived at the clearing house and the debit or credit position of the bank is determined. These are booked in their current accounts maintained by the settling bank. This represents the inter-bank settlement. The settlement of funds between the service branch and the branch concerned represents the transfer of funds to the branch level. The payment process is completed only when the funds are debited from the drawer's account and credited to the payee's account. This occurs after the completion of the return clearing mentioned earlier.

Return Clearing: Realisation of a cheque i.e. payment occurs after the cheque that is returned unpaid takes place in this clearing. The aggregate of all items unpaid is debited to the original presenting bank and credited to the drawee bank. The same process is mirrored in the inter-branch settlement at the service branch of a bank. The credit given to the payee on account of the cheque is reversed.

Inter-branch Clearing: Cheques presented by customers drawn on different branches of the same bank need not be sent to the clearing house as the transfer of funds is internal to the bank. The service branch usually acts as a settlement branch for the branches and the instruments are sent to the drawee branches while the inter-branch accounts are credited or debited internally.

Time Lag: The total clearing cycle including the return clearing introduces a time lag in the payments process. The need for physical presentment of the cheque at the branch where it is drawn on, requires the movement of cheques from one place to another. As a result, the recipient of payment has to wait until the collecting banker is fully satisfied that the cheque has been paid. This time lag will continue irrespective of the level of technology and improvements in process, so long as the physical presentment of the cheque is necessary as per the banking law.

Collection of Outstation Instruments: As the clearing jurisdiction is local, a separate procedure has evolved for the collection of cheques drawn on banks outside the clearing house area. In this case, the cheques are sent by post for collection to the representative branch or correspondent branch for presentation in the clearing house in the outstation centre. Once the cheque is realised, the proceeds are remitted to the original presenting bank for credit to the customer account. This leads to a significant delay in the payment of these cheques and there is considerable uncertainty regarding the time of realisation. The National Clearing system, described elsewhere, has considerably reduced the time taken for realisation at designated centres.

Settlement of Funds for Outstation Items: Due to delays in collection of outstation cheques, various alternative forms of payments instruments are widely used to settle outstation payments. Some of the payment items such as demand drafts, "payable at par" warrants etc., have been described in the previous chapter. In all these cases, whether cheques or drafts, the question of settlement between paying bank and the collecting bank remains. In the case of demand drafts, the payment is usually internal to the bank and is settled by book transfers using an internal pipe line account maintained in the bank. In the case of 'At par' items, a single account maintained in any branch is debited and various paying branches are paid. Sometimes the layers of intermediation increase as the funds move from a paying bank to its branch at other centre to a collecting bank at that centre. In all these cases, the delays involved in the payments transaction are considerable both for the recipient of the funds as also for the banks involved.

Prior to 1986, there were no formal regulations and rules governing the transaction of business in the clearing houses. Each Clearing House had its own rules and regulations based on local conventions and convenience. In case of disputes, problem resolution proved to be a tricky exercise.

In 1986, Reserve Bank of India framed a set of guidelines known as the Uniform Regulations and Rules (URR) for the Bankers' Clearing Houses. These guidelines were prescribed against the backdrop of considerable changes occurring in the functioning of the clearing houses due to the introduction of computerisation in the banking industry.

The Regulations are designed to provide a uniform framework for the conduct of clearing throughout the country and have been adopted individually by the general body of each clearing house in the country. Individual Clearing Houses are free to frame their own rules consistent with the broad framework provided by the Regulations.

The Uniform Rules and Regulations represent a significant step forward in providing a formal institutional framework for the payments system in the country. They govern the conduct of the clearing business, prescribe a fair membership criteria and provide for penalties in the case of default. They also explicitly provide for significant oversight function for Reserve Bank of India.

The Regulations provide for an ex-officio President of the clearing house, who is the officer-in-charge of the bank managing the clearing house. The President is assisted by a Standing Committee comprising of a few representatives of member banks to help him resolve urgent problems.

All banks including State Co-operative banks, General Post Offices are eligible to become members of the clearing house.

The Regulations stipulate the maximum value of daily presentations that can be made in the clearing by private commercial banks, central co-operative banks and primary co-operative banks, with reference to their deposit liabilities. The presentation limits, at 10% of the deposit liabilities (which could be relaxed in genuine cases) for each year are fixed on the basis of the deposit liabilities of the previous year. This is a risk control measure introduced to maintain stability in the payments system. This is also an attempt at introducing a measure of stability in the payments system by limiting the volatility of payments demand.

The Rules provide for Hours of Clearing and Return of Documents. Based on the needs of the members as also local trade and consumer associations, a clearing house may decide on the number of presentation clearings and corresponding return clearings. The jurisdiction of the clearing house i.e., the number of branches covered is specified by the President of the Clearing House and advised to all members and sub-members.

The Rules lay down clear procedures for settlement of clearing transactions. These include resolving payable and receivable differences, prescribing a minimum balance to be kept with the bank managing the Clearing House and penalties for defaulting in maintaining the minimum balance and the overdraft, if any, due to adverse clearing position.

URR prescribe the mechanism to be followed in settlement in the event of default by a member in meeting its clearing liabilities. In the event of default, all the instruments drawn on the defaulting bank are withdrawn from the settlement process and settlement is effected as if the defaulting bank did not participate in the clearing. All credit due to the bank in respect of the instruments presented by it in the clearing is held in a suspense account and the amount of such instruments returned unpaid is debited to the Suspense account. The balance if any is credited to the defaulting member.

Settlement activities in India are dispersed through the 860 clearing houses in the country. However, the banks need to maintain liquidity or remit funds to settle their clearing obligations at any or all of the centres of their activity. Surplus funds may be available with a bank at any one centre after the settlement operations are carried out and these funds may need to be transferred to a deficit funds centre. The bank with surplus funds may wish to deploy its surplus funds in a profitable manner in the inter-bank or call money market. A remittance facility therefore, is required to facilitate transfer of funds from one place to another.

The Reserve Bank is the banker to the Central and State Governments. Tax collections and revenue receipts gathered across the country need to be credited to the Government account at Central Accounts Section (CAS), Nagpur. Similar is the case with the proceeds of Treasury Bill auctions. Funds transfer arrangements between banks, between government accounts and the RBI offices would therefore, be essential to take care of the needs of the payments and settlement process.

Remittance Facilities Scheme: Reserve Bank of India operates an integrated Remittance Facilities Scheme (RFS) to enable funds transfer between the banks. The RFS Scheme, which came into being on October 1, 1940, facilitates funds transfer between different centres in the country in an expeditious manner with minimum costs. The Scheme is operated by Reserve Bank of India and its agents (banks) including treasuries and sub-treasuries. In other centres, the SBI operates a remittance scheme to enable banks to fund and withdraw from various settlement accounts. In the absence of the SBI, its associate banks or the public sector bank managing the clearing house, provide remittance facility. This enables the movement of settlement funds between all the clearing centres.

There are no limits on the amounts that can be transferred under the RFS in the case of the Reserve Bank and the agencies. Limits have however, been prescribed for issue and encashment of remittances at treasuries. The Central and State governments are entitled to remit funds free of charge throughout the country. In the case of banks, certain charges have been prescribed, as also the minimum amounts which can be remitted.

Payment and Settlement Systems

Increasing Funds Transfers by the CBC Wire

The two main subsystems under the CBC wire are the CBC Interbank Fund-transfer Settlement System (CIFS), and the Central Government Securities Settlement System (CGSS). The CIFS launched in May 1995 is an on-line, large-value funds transfer system. Since September 2002, the system has been operated in a real-time gross settlement (RTGS) basis. Participants of the CIFS include banks, investment and trust companies, and bills finance companies.

For those who maintain transaction accounts with the Bank, they may directly use the CIFS to transfer funds. Payment instructions are also sent over the CIFS for settling obligations on check clearing, adjusting reserve account balances, or making payments associated with interbank loans, bill transactions, and bond transactions. For the year 2005, the total value of funds transfered by the system grew by 27.2 percent from 2004 to NT$246,279 billion.

Established in September 1997, the CGSS is a real-time gross settlement system for the issuance, transfer, redemption, and interest payment of book-entry central government securities. Currently, the book-entry transactions of central government securities within a clearing bank can be made on a delivery-versus-payment (DVP) basis while those between clearing banks cannot. To reduce the settlement risk in interbank transactions, the Bank plans to link the CGSS with the CIFS to allow clearing banks to handle these settlements on a DVP basis as well.

Declining Check Clearing by the Clearing House System

Supervised by the Bank, the Taiwan Clearing House System handles the clearing and settlement of checks, promissory notes, and drafts among banks. Participants of the system include banks, credit co-operative associations, as well as credit departments of farmers' and fishermen's associations. All financial institutions in Taiwan using these facilities should hold reserve accounts at the Bank. The Bank also participates in this System.

The Taiwan Clearing House (TCH) is responsible for the operation of the system. In order to promote the efficiency of check clearing and to facilitate funds management for enterprises, the Bank guided the TCH to enhance its computerized check-clearing operation. Through dividing Taiwan into north, middle and south exchange regions, the checks collected by clearing houses were exchanged in three processing centers located in Taipei, Taichung and Kaohsiung, respectively.

The Bank then handles the final settlement for these processing centers. This quasi-centralized and electronic processing system is conducive to time-saving for check processing and reducing manual handling loads. It also facilitates funds management of both financial institutions and enterprises.

Both the volume and value of TCH transactions have been decreasing over the past few years. In 2005, checks and bills settled by the TCH system amounted to NT$23,961 billion, a decrease of 9.9 percent from 2004, mainly due to the growth of interbank remittance transactions.

Increasing Transactions through the FISC Interbank Payment System

The Interbank Remittance System (IRS), launched in August 1987 and operated by the Financial Information Service Co., Ltd (FISC), is the largest retail electronic payment system in the country. This system provides remittance services to the general public, government agencies, and banks.

Credit cards and ATM (automatic teller machine) cards are the most popular payment cards in the country. The interbank settlements of credit card transactions between card-issuing banks and retail merchant's banks are mostly made by the FISC. The CD/ATM (cash dispenser/ automatic teller machine) System, which provides 24-hour cross-bank withdrawal, balance inquiry, funds transfer, credit card cash advance, and IC card loading services, is also operated by the FISC. All the participants in the IRS can join the system. In addition, the FISC handles funds transfers for on-batch payments, debit cards, electronic and mobile banking, etc.

In 2005, the FISC handled a total value of NT$107,166 billion in funds transactions, a moderate increase of 2.5 percent from the previous year.

Is the Gold Standard Still the Gold Standard among Monetary Systems?

Critics have raised a number of theoretical and historical objections to the gold standard. Some have called the gold standard a "crazy" idea. The gold standard is not a flawless monetary system. Neither is the fiat money alternative. In light of historical evidence about the comparative magnitude of these flaws, however, the gold standard is a policy option that deserves serious consideration.

In a study covering many decades in a large sample of countries, Federal Reserve Bank economists found that "money growth and inflation are higher" under fiat standards than under gold and silver standards. Nor is the gold standard a source of harmful deflation. Alan Greenspan has testified before Congress that "a central bank properly functioning will endeavor to, in many cases, replicate what a gold standard would itself generate."

This study addresses the leading criticisms of the gold standard, relating to the costs of gold, the costs of transition, the dangers of speculation, and the need for a lender of last resort. One criticism is found to have some merit. The United States would not enjoy the benefits of being on an international gold standard if it were the first and only country whose currency was linked to gold.

A gold standard does not guarantee perfect steadiness in the growth of the money supply, but historical comparison shows that it has provided more moderate and steadier money growth in practice than the present-day alternative, politically empowering a central banking committee to determine growth in the stock of fiat money. From the perspective of limiting money growth appropriately, the gold standard is far from a crazy idea.

For the first time in many years, the monetary arrangements of the United States have become an issue in the 2008 presidential race. The subprime crisis and the decline in the foreign exchange value of the dollar have raised questions about the performance of the Federal Reserve Board. One candidate has proposed ending the post-1971 experiment with an unanchored fiat dollar issued by the Federal Reserve and returning to a gold standard with private money issue. Critics have raised a number of theoretical and historical objections to the gold standard. Some have called the gold standard a "crazy" idea.

The overall intent of this paper is to make practical institutional comparisons, warts and all. The gold standard is not a flawless monetary system. Neither is the fiat money alternative. The gold standard is most certainly not a crazy idea. It is a policy option that deserves serious consideration.

"The gold standard" generically means a monetary system in which a certain mass of gold defines the monetary unit (e.g., the dollar) and serves as the ultimate medium of redemption. For example, during the "classical" gold standard period (1879-1914), the U.S. dollar was defined as 0.048 troy oz. of pure gold. Inverting the defined ratio, one ounce of pure gold was equivalent to US$20.67. Gold coins need not, and historically did not, form the predominant medium of exchange.

Issuers of paper currency and checkable deposits, normally private commercial banks but also a government central bank if one exists, make their notes redeemable for gold and hold gold coins and bullion as reserves for meeting redemption demands. Because of the banks' contractual obligation to redeem in gold, the volume of paper currency and deposits-the everyday means of payment-is geared to the volume of gold.

Key Objections

"A gold standard leaves the quantity of money to be determined by accidental forces." There is a germ of truth to this concern. A gold standard does leave the quantity and purchasing power of money to be determined by the forces of supply and demand in the market for gold. There can be "accidental" shifts in the supply and demand curves to which the quantity and purchasing power of money will respond. Our current fiat standard, by contrast, leaves the supply of money to the decisions of a committee (namely, the Federal Open Market Committee of the Federal Reserve

System). The practical question is: under which system are the quantity and purchasing power of money better behaved?

As is well known, the stock of gold did not grow at a perfectly steady rate during the era of the historical gold standard. Some increases in gold output-such as the Yukon discoveries and the development of the cyanide process-were responses to previous increases in demand and the purchasing power of gold, and thus helped to stabilize the purchasing power of gold over the long run. Other increases resulted from accidental discoveries.

The largest such "supply shock" in the 19th century was the 1848 discovery of gold in California. The California gold rush meant that more ounces would be mined at any given purchasing power cf gold. The outpouring of gold from California reduced the purchasing power of gold around the world, or in other words, generated an inflation of the price level. But how large an inflation? The magnitude was surprisingly small. Even over the most inflationary interval, the general price index (the GDP deflator) for the United States rose from 5.71 in 1849 (year 2000 = 100) to 6.42 in 1857, an increase of 12.4 percent spread over eight years. The compound annual price inflation rate over those eight years was slightly less than 1.5 percent. Twenty-two years later, when the gold standard was finally restored following its suspension during the Civil War, the purchasing power of gold had actually risen slightly (the price level was slightly lower).

The economic historian Hugh Rockoff, in an examination of the output of gold, concluded that "it is fair to describe the fluctuations in the supply of gold under the classical standard as small and well-timed." He found that supply of fiat money in the postwar period (1949-79), by contrast to the behavior of gold under the classical gold standard, had both higher annual rates of growth and a higher standard deviation of annual growth rates around decade averages.

In a study covering many decades in a large sample of countries, the Federal Reserve Bank of Minneapolis economists Arthur Rolnick and Warren Weber4 similarly found that "money growth and inflation are higher" under fiat standards than under gold and silver standards. Specifically, they reported that the average inflation rate for the fiat standard observations is 9.17 percent per year; the average inflation rate for the commodity standard observations is 1.75 percent per year.

This result was not driven by a few extreme cases; in fact, in computing the average rates of inflation Rolnick and Weber deliberately omitted cases of hyperinflation (which occurred only under fiat money). Still, they noted, every country in our sample experienced a higher rate of inflation in the period during which it was operating under a fiat standard than in the period during which it was operating under a commodity standard.

The evidence thus indicates that growth in the stock of gold has been slower and steadier in practice than growth in the stock of fiat money. Of course, U.S. inflation is thankfully not as high as 9 percent today, but at 4.3 percent (consumer price index, year-over-year) it is currently more than twice as high as Rolnick and Weber's figure for commodity standards. Correspondingly, the purchasing power of money under the gold standard was steadier and more predictable. The greater reliability of the purchasing power of the monetary unit under the gold standard was reflected in a thicker market for long-term corporate bonds than exists today. Under a gold standard, the price level can be trusted not to wander far over the next 30 years because it is constrained by impersonal market forces. Any sizable price level increase (fall in the purchasing power of gold) caused by a reduced demand to hold gold would reduce the quantity of gold mined, thereby reversing the price level movement. Conversely, any sizable price level decrease (rise in the purchasing power of gold) caused by an increased demand to hold gold would increase the quantity mined, thereby reversing that price level movement. Under a fiat standard, the future price level depends on the personalities of yet-to-be-appointed monetary authorities and thus is anybody's guess.

The blogger Megan McArdle thus gets things almost exactly backward when she writes: "The gold standard cannot do what a well-run fiat currency can do, which is to tailor the money supply to the economy's demand for money." Under the gold standard, market forces do in fact automatically tailor the money supply to the economy's demand for money.

The economics of gold mining operates to match world supply with world demand at the stable price level (though admittedly large demand shocks can take years to be accommodated), while the "Price-specie-Flow mechanism" quickly brings gold from the rest of the world into any single country where demand for money has grown. We can only imagine a well-run fiat-currency-issuing central bank trying to match these properties. We cannot observe any central bank that has actually managed it. Peter Bernholz, for example, tells us that "a study of about 30 currencies shows that there has not been a single case of a currency freely manipulated by its government or central bank since 1700 which enjoyed price stability for at least 30 years running."

Some critics have posed absurd-case scenarios, such as "What if some alchemist turns lead into gold?" and "What if a golden meteorite hit the earth?" But these are of no more actual relevance than "What if the Federal Reserve chairman becomes insane?" "A gold standard would be a source of harmful deflation." The inflation rate under the gold standard averaged close to zero over generations, sometimes slightly positive and sometimes slightly negative over individual decades. Rolnick and Weber, as quoted above, found an average inflation rate of 1.75 percent over the sample of gold and silver episodes reported in the published version of their paper; an earlier version using a different sample arrived at an average rate of-0.5 percent. In 1879 the United States resumed gold redemption for the U.S. dollar, which had been suspended since the Civil War. Between 1880 and 1900 the United States experienced one of the most prolonged periods of deflation on record.

The price level trended more or less steadily downward, beginning at 6.10 and ending at 5.49 (GDP deflator, base year 2000 = 100). That works out to a total decline of 10 percent stretched over 20 years. The deflationary period was no disaster for the real economy. Real output per capita began the period at $3,379 and ended it at $4,943 (both in 2000 dollars). Total real per capita growth was thus a morethan-healthy 46 percent. (Real GDP itself more than doubled.)

Monetary economists distinguish a benign deflation (due to the output of goods growing rapidly while the stock of money grows slowly, as in the 1880-1900 period) from a harmful deflation (due to unanticipated shrinkage in the money stock). The gold standard was a source of mild benign deflation in periods when the output of goods grew faster than the stock of gold. Prices particularly fell for those goods whose production enjoyed great technological improvement (for example oil and steel after 1880).

Strong growth of real output, for particular goods or in general, cannot be considered harmful.

It would be possible for the central bank under a fiat money standard to offset productivity-driven declines in some prices by expanding the quantity of money in order to drive others prices upward, thus eliminating deflation "on average." But there is no social benefit in doing so. Falling costs of production in steel (i.e. productivity gains) do not discourage investment in steel. A gradual anticipated deflation does not discourage investment, especially not when productivity gains are driving growth in the first place.

Nor does a deflation penalize debtors once it comes to be anticipated, because nominal interest rates adjust downward to reflect anticipated repayment in dollars of higher purchasing power.

"The gold standard was responsible for the U.S. banking panics of the late 19th century and for the monetary contraction of 1929-33 and, thereby, for the Great Depression." The U.S. monetary contraction of 1929-33 is the prime example of a harmful deflation. It should be noted that it happened on the Federal Reserve's watch. The episode should not be blamed on the gold standard, but on the combination of a weak banking system and a befuddled central bank. The U.S. banking system was prone to runs and panics in the late 19th century and continued to be so through the 1929-33 episode in which the Fed stood by and did not supply replacement reserves to keep the money stock from contracting.

Other countries on the gold standard-Canada, for example-had no banking panic in 1929-33 (nor did Canada have panics in the late 19th century), so the gold standard couldn't have been responsible for the panics. Rather the panics were due to completely avoidable legal restrictions (namely the ban on branch banking and compulsory bond collateral requirements that make the supply of banknotes "inelastic") that weakened the U.S. banking system.

"The benefit of a gold standard (restraining inflation) is attainable at less cost by properly controlling the supply of fiat money." Although growth in the stock of fiat money could in principle be as slow (or slower) than growth in the stock of gold under a gold standard, it has not been so in practice, as already noted.

Alan Greenspan actually used to recommend controlling the fiat money supply to mimic the price-level behavior of a gold standard. In response to questioning at a 2001 congressional hearing, Greenspan said: "Mr. Chairman, so long as you have fiat currency, which is a statutory issue, a central bank properly functioning will endeavor to, in many cases, replicate what a gold standard would itself generate." Two years later he added that central banks had created the inflation of the 1970s because the gold standard no longer constrained them, but they had been able to bring inflation back down by belatedly learning to emulate the restrained money growth that was characteristic of the gold standard:

The general wisdom during the period subsequent to the 1930s was that as we moved to an essentially fiat money standard, that there was no anchor to the general price level. And indeed, what we subsequently observed is, as you point out, a very marked increase in general price levels, indeed, around the world as we removed ourselves from commodity standards, and specifically gold. I had always thought that the fiat money system was chronically and inevitably an inflation vehicle, and indeed, said so repeatedly. I have been quite surprised, and I must say pleased, by the fact that central bankers have been able to effectively simulate many of the characteristics of the gold standard by constraining the degree of finance in a manner which effectively has brought down general price levels.

Fiat money regimes have not, however, accomplished price stability as fully as did the gold standard. Although inflation is less severe today than it was 30 years ago, experienced inflation rates, and the expectations of future inflation rates embodied in long-term interest rates, have remained higher than corresponding rates under the classical gold standard. It is true that a commodity money standard entails a resource cost (sometimes described as "digging up gold just to bury it in bank vaults"). So does the production of bicycle locks from metal rather than paper. The resource cost of a gold standard has often been exaggerated by estimates that assume 100 percent gold backing for all forms of money. The preeminent monetary economist Milton

Friedman, during the 1950s and 1960s, relied on such an estimate in judging a well-run fiat standard more efficient than a commodity standard. Friedman overestimated the resource costs of a gold standard by assuming-although such a system has no advocates and no historical precedent-100 percent reserves against all components of M2 (that is, against even time deposits). With a historically more reasonable fractional reserve ratio of 2 percent, the amount of gold needed in vaults and thus the resource cost of a gold standard shrinks by a factor of 50.

Friedman wanted to substitute for gold a less costly paper money standard bound by a strict money growth rule. But in the 1980s he changed his mind about the feasibility of getting the Fed to commit to anything of the sort, reconsidered the costs of inflation in the absence of a strict rule,14 and began to call for abolishing the Federal Reserve System (though not replacing it with a gold standard, because he thought no government would any longer consent to be constrained by a gold standard).

Abolishing the Fed may be a pipe dream, but for those who have that dream a gold standard may be the most plausible way of abolishing the Fed. As Greenspan recently explained to Daily Show host Jon Stewart, under a gold standard a central bank is unnecessary. "A gold standard is no restraint at all, because government can devalue or suspend gold redemption whenever it wants." A similar claim could be made about any (other) restraint in the Constitution. And yet constitutional rules are useful. By authorizing only a limited set of government activities, ruling others simply out of bounds, they save the public the trouble of trying to weigh every potential activity on a cost-benefit basis. An important problem in fiat money regimes, as famously identified by Finn Kydland and Edward C. Prescott, is the lack of an enforceable commitment not to use surprise monetary expansion and resulting inflation as a temporary stimulus to the economy.

When the public knows that the central bank would be tempted to use surprise inflation, the public rationally expects higher-than-optimal-inflation. The central bank has to deliver higher-than-optimal inflation to avoid a negative surprise. An unfortunate standoff is reached at a higher-than-optimal inflation rate (which, being fully anticipated, provides no economic stimulus). A gold standard avoids that trap.

Like tying Ulysses to the mast, it achieves better results by removing the option (to use surprise inflation) that leads to ruin. Of course, a gold standard is not the only possible rule for constraining the creation of money. Alternatives include a Friedman-type money-growth rule, or an inflation targeting rule. But the gold standard has a longer history, and is the only historically tested rule that does not presuppose a central bank.

Leaving money issue in the hands of private banks rather than a government institution, as the United States did before 1913, removes the option to use surprise monetary expansion one step further. It remains true that government can suspend the gold standard in an emergency, as both sides did during the Civil War, but the spirit of the gold standard calls for returning to the parity afterward, as did the United States. Judging by longterm interest rates and the thick market for long-term bonds under the post-bellum classical gold standard, the risk of permanent devaluation or suspension was considered small.

"A gold standard, like any fixed exchange-rate system, is vulnerable to speculative attacks." What opens the door to speculative attacks is a weak commitment to the existing parity, whether in gold or any other reserve currency. A central bank's commitment can be weak, and that is indeed a problem when combining a gold standard with central banking. Fortunately, a gold standard doesn't require a central bank. With decentralized private money issue, there is no institution capable of devaluing, so there is no danger of speculative attacks on the parity. A gold standard free of a central bank provides a commitment to non-inflation made good by the impersonal economics of gold mining (for gold itself) and by enforceable redemption contracts and the competitive market value of reputation (for bank-issued money).

"Fiat money is necessary so that a lender of last resort can meet the liquidity needs of the banking system." History shows that a lender of last resort would hardly be needed, given a stable monetary regime and a sound banking system (again it is instructive to contrast the United States with Canada in the 19th century). In the rare cases such a lender might be needed, bank clearinghouses could play the role.

"Switching to a gold standard would involve massive transition costs." The transition cost involved in reestablishing a gold definition for the dollar would be small. Unlike with Europe's transition to the euro, price tags and bank accounts would not need to be redenominated because the name "dollar" would be retained. At the right reentry rate, dollar prices would not need to jump. "We must have gone off the gold standard in the first place for good reasons." In 1933, President Franklin D. Roosevelt devalued from $20.67 to $35 per troy ounce of gold as a means to re-inflate the dollar price level. But the (harmful) money stock shrinkage and price deflation of 1929-33 hadn't been due to a loss of gold.

It had been due to a collapse of weak U.S. banks. The deflation could have been remedied by better monetary policy and banking reform without going off gold. In 1971, Nixon shut the gold window because the Federal Reserve had expanded the stock of dollars too much to maintain the $35 per ounce parity. Nixon's action could have been avoided had the Fed not expanded the stock of dollars so much in the 1960s. It was not the rules of the gold standard that had failed. It was, rather, the Fed that had failed to abide by the rules of the gold standard.

"The gold standard is an example of price-fixing by government." The gold standard doesn't fix a price between dollars and gold any more than the traditional British measurement system fixes a price between pints and quarts. The fixed relationship is a matter of definition. A gold standard defines the dollar (or whatever the name of the monetary unit) as a specified mass of gold. Dollars are not separate goods from gold.

"A gold standard would allow Putin to buy the United States." Any Russian autocrat's ability to use the proceeds from Russian gold mines to buy American assets would be no greater under a gold standard than it is today, unless the purchasing power of gold were to rise. And there is no good reason to think that would happen. The real purchasing power of gold today, under fiat money, is higher than it was before 1971, in large part because people are hoarding gold as a hedge against fiat money inflation. The current fiat system is enriching Putin more than a gold standard would. "There isn't enough gold." There is necessarily enough gold to support enough dollars to support today's dollar price level (or whatever price level is desired), at the right gold definition of the dollar.

"The United States can't recreate the classical international gold standard by itself." I have saved for last what I think is the strongest objection to unilateral return to gold on the part of the United States. The nation would not enjoy the benefits of being on an international gold standard if it were the first and only country whose currency was linked to gold. At least two major benefits would be missing: (1) the United States would not enjoy fixed exchange rates with the rest of the world, and (2) the purchasing power of gold would not be as stable.

The purchasing power (or relative price) of today's demonetized gold has been much less stable than that of gold under the 19th century's global gold standard, because demand to hold gold today is largely a speculative rather than a transactions demand. With only one economy on gold-albeit a large economy-monetary use of gold would likely remain the tail rather than the dog. Thus even in the unlikely event that the United States were to elect a president committed to a pro-gold policy, that president would be prudent to try to cultivate similar commitments from the governments of the other leading economies of the world before taking us down the yellow brick road alone.

CONCLUSION

Under the gold standard the issue of common money by banks is restrained by the cost of acquiring gold, which is determined by impersonal supply and demand forces in the goldmining market. Because of the issuers' contractual obligations to redeem in gold, and corresponding prudential need to hold gold reserves, the dollar volume of paper currency and deposits-the stock of money-is geared to the volume of gold. Growth in the stock of money is governed by market forces rather than by government fiat. A gold standard does not guarantee perfect steadiness in the growth of the money supply, but historical comparison shows that it has provided more moderate and steadier money growth in practice than the present-day alternative, politically empowering a central banking committee to determine growth in the stock of fiat money. From the perspective of limiting money growth appropriately, the gold standard is far from a crazy idea.

Historical problems of U.S. banking instability, sometimes blamed on the gold standard, turn out on closer inspection to have had been rooted in banking regulations that inadvertently weakened U.S. banks. Gold standard countries like Canada that avoided the peculiar banking restrictions of the United States (namely the ban on branch banking and compulsory bond collateral requirements that make the supply of banknotes "inelastic") also avoided the instability. As we discovered in the greatest banking panic, that of 1929-33, having a Federal Reserve System capable of overriding the gold standard did not eliminate the problem of weakness in the U.S. banking system. Other supposed historical problems, like price deflation due to goods production outgrowing gold production, turn out not to have been actual problems.

A gold standard does entail resource costs of mining the gold that is lodged in bank vaults. But so too does a fiat standard entail resource costs, primarily in the form of the deadweight costs of inflation. All in all, because the costs of a gold standard are reasonably small in relation to its benefits, the gold standard is not a crazy idea.

7

Recent Developments in Discount Window Policy

Underlying trends in the depository sector along with changes in federal legislation have had impor-tant ramifications in recent years for the discount window, the Federal Reserve's lending facility. The periods of stress and consolidation in the depository sector during the 1980s and 1990s led to the active involvement of the discount window in many failing-bank situations. Indeed, the scope of problems in the banking industry and the extent of discount window lending to troubled institutions were greater than in any period since the Great Depression.

In addition, changes became evident during the 1980s in the willingness of healthy institutions to turn to the discount window. Many banks appar-ently became more reluctant to turn to the window for fear of provoking market concerns about their financial condition.

The greater reluctance to borrow weakened the historical relationship between discount window borrowing and the spread of the federal funds rate over the discount rate. This weakening, in turn, impaired the effec-tiveness of the discount window in tempering unexpected pressure in the reserve market and reduced the Federal Reserve's emphasis on bor-rowed reserves in the day-to-day management of the reserve market.

Perhaps the most notable legislation affecting the discount window has been the Depository Institu-tions Deregulation and Monetary Control Act of 1980, which dramatically expanded the universe of depository institutions eligible to borrow at the discount window. As a result, the Federal Reserve assumed greater direct responsibility for respond-ing to the liquidity needs of all depositories.

Another important legislative change arose in response to the large number of bank failures in the 1980s and the associated depletion of the insurance funds of the Federal Deposit Insurance Corporation (FDIC). The legislation, the Federal Deposit Insur-ance Corporation Improvement Act of 1991, con-tained provisions intended to discourage Federal Reserve lending to depositories that do not meet minimum capital standards. Although these provi-sions do not prohibit the Federal Reserve from lending to such institutions, they specify that the Federal Reserve will incur a limited liability to the FDIC for lending that extends beyond certain time periods and that results in increased losses to the FDIC's insurance funds.

DISCOUNT WINDOW LENDING: THE BASICS

Sections 10B and 13 of the Federal Reserve Act authorize the Federal Reserve Banks to extend discount window credit to depository institutions in the form of discounts and advances. In the early years of the Federal Reserve System, discounts were the primary form of discount window credit. A bank wishing to obtain a discount from its Fed-eral Reserve Bank would present a short-term busi-ness loan or other asset meeting the type and matu-rity specifications set forth in the Federal Reserve Act.

The Federal Reserve Bank would extend credit in an amount that reflected the value of the asset at maturity minus a "discount" based on the Federal Reserve's discount rate and the time until maturity of the asset. When the asset matured, the Federal Reserve returned it to the bank and received from the bank a cash payment equal to the maturity value of the asset.

An advance is operationally simpler than a dis-count, and all discount window credit has been provided in the form of advances for many years. For an advance, a bank requests a loan from its Federal Reserve Bank. The rate charged on the loan is the discount rate, and the duration of the loan is determined by the Reserve Bank.

To secure the advance, the borrower must pledge collateral in amounts and of types that are satisfactory to the lending Reserve Bank.

In addition to authorizing loans to "eligible" depository institutions, the Federal Reserve Act-in sections 13(3) and 13(13)-authorizes the System to act in emergency circumstances as "lender of last resort" to individuals, partnerships, and corporations. Enacted in 1932, section 13(3) was intended to enable the Federal Reserve to provide credit in the form of discounts for borrow-ers unable to obtain adequate credit accommoda-tions from other banking institutions; its use was limited to periods of unusual and exigent circum-stances, as determined by the affirmative vote of at least five members of the Board of Governors.

The Congress enacted section 13(13) in 1933 to authorize the Federal Reserve to make advances to individuals, partnerships, and corporations on the security of U.S. Treasury and federal agency obligations. Although this provision, unlike sec-tion 13(3), carries no statutory restrictions on its use, the Federal Reserve has always regarded its applicability as being limited to unusual or excep-tional circumstances. Indeed, since 1973, the Board's Regulation A, which governs discount window lending activities, has restricted use of this authority to emergency circumstances in which borrowers cannot obtain credit from other sources and their failure to obtain credit would adversely affect the economy.

PURPOSE AND BORROWING ELIGIBILITY

The Federal Reserve Board's Regulation A defines three discount window programs, each serving a distinct purpose: (1) adjustment credit, to help depository institutions meet unexpected short-term liquidity needs; (2) seasonal credit, to assist smaller institutions in managing liquidity needs that arise from regular swings in loans and deposits; and (3) extended credit, to help depositories that have somewhat longer-term liquidity needs resulting from exceptional circumstances. None of these programs is intended to be a substitute for market funding sources; Regulation A stipulates that banks must first exhaust market sources of funds before turning to the discount window.

To ensure that this principle is met in practice, Reserve Banks regularly monitor the sources and uses of funds for institutions while they are borrowing. Before the Monetary Control Act of 1980, only banks that were members of the Federal Reserve System had regular access to discount window credit.

The act imposed reserve requirements on a much larger set of depository institutions and simultaneously extended discount window access to them.

As a result, nonmember commercial banks and savings banks as well as savings and loan associations (S&Ls) and credit unions became eligible to borrow at the discount window.

An institution that anticipates borrowing from the Federal Reserve must execute a borrowing agreement and other documents with its Federal Reserve Bank that define the terms and conditions under which discount window loans will be pro-vided.

For both historical and administrative rea-sons, most institutions that are eligible to borrow do not choose to file borrowing agreements or borrow at the discount window. For example, of the approximately 27,000 depository institutions eligible to borrow at the beginning of this year, only about 7,000 had filed borrowing agreements. Many smaller banks-turn to their correspondent banks when funding needs arise. In addition, spe-cial industry lenders such as the Federal Home Loan Banks and corporate central credit unions serve as sources of liquidity assistance for their member institutions; credit unions, in particular, elect to rely almost entirely on their corporate central credit unions for any liquidity assistance rather than turn to the Federal Reserve.

The Mechanics of Borrowing

Institutions almost always initiate loan requests by a telephone call to their respective Reserve Banks. During the call, the borrower describes the nature of the funding shortfall and indicates the amount and duration of the loan required.

Staff members at the Reserve Bank ensure that the institution has filed the necessary borrowing documents and has collateral to secure the loan fully. Satisfactory collateral may include U.S. government and agency securities, mortgages covering one-to four-family residences, state and local government securities, commercial and consumer loans, and other cus-tomer notes of acceptable quality.

Many institutions that anticipate a periodic need to borrow maintain a pool of collateral earmarked to secure discount window loans. Collateral is usually held at the Federal Reserve Banks or by acceptable third-party custodians, but borrowers in good financial condition may be permitted to hold their own collateral under terms and conditions established by the Reserve Banks. The face value of collateral pledged to secure a discount window loan generally exceeds the amount of the loan; the difference is intended to provide a cushion against loss in the event that a borrower defaults and the Federal Reserve is forced to liquidate the collateral.

THE ADJUSTMENT CREDIT PROGRAM

The adjustment credit program operates at a "micro" level by assisting individual depository institutions in meeting temporary funding require-ments in appropriate circumstances. The program also operates at a "macro" level by moderating unexpected pressures in the reserve market.

Lending Policies

Regulation A establishes two key criteria for determining whether to approve a request for adjustment credit: The loan must be for an appropriate reason and borrowers must have exhausted all reasonably available alternative sources of funds, including credit from special industry lenders. Discount offic-ers at each Reserve Bank necessarily use their own judgment in applying these principles to individual circumstances. Appropriate reasons for borrowing include temporary, unanticipated funding short-falls. Inappropriate reasons for borrowing include funding a planned increase in loans or securities, meeting an anticipated runoff of higher-cost funds, and exploiting the spread of the federal funds rate over the discount rate.

In judging whether borrowers have pursued all reasonably available alternative sources of funds before turning to the discount window, the Federal Reserve distinguishes between banks with ready access to national money markets, usually large banks, and those that do not have such access, which generally are smaller banks. The distinction between large and small banks is not, however, based solely on asset or deposit size.

Most U.S. branches of foreign banks, for example, are treated as large institutions even when the quantity of their assets booked in the United States is small; these branches are typically part of large multinational banking organizations that have ready access to market sources of funds, and the parent entities are expected to meet the bulk of the funding needs of their U.S. branches. Under these distinctions, Reserve Banks typi-cally grant the requests of large banks for discount window- assistance only very late in the day, when the money markets are closing, and usually only when money markets have tightened considerably near the end of a reserve maintenance period. In addition, the largest banks are assumed to be in a position to repay their discount window loans quickly through prompt adjustments in their balance.

As a result, discount window loans to large banks are usually extended for only one busi-ness day. Banks with less ready access to money market funding may request discount window loans on any day of the reserve maintenance period and at an earlier hour of the day; the Reserve Banks may approve such loans with a term of several days.

The interest rate charged for adjustment credit ordinarily is the basic discount rate. In certain circumstances, however, a higher rate may be applied. For an unusually large loan that results from a major operating problem at the borrower's facility, the highest rate established for loans to depository institutions may be charged; in the current discount rate structure, that rate would be the market-related rate on extended credit.

The Borrowing Function

Apart from assisting individual banks in meeting short-term liquidity pressures, adjustment credit serves an important "pressure release" function in the reserve market. The level of adjustment bor-rowing has historically exhibited a fairly stable relationship to the spread of the federal funds rate over the discount rate; wider spreads create a greater incentive to borrow, thus leading to higher aggregate levels of borrowing. This so-called "borrowing function" works to dilute the influence that shifts in the supply and demand for reserves can have on the federal funds rate. For example, on a given day, changes in factors affect-ing the supply of nonborrowed reserves, such as increases in currency in circulation or flows of reserves from depository institutions to the U.S. Treasury's account at the Federal Reserve, could result in an aggregate shortage of reserves available to depository institutions. A shortage of reserves tends to push up the federal funds rate. But a rise in the federal funds rate induces more banks to turn to the discount window, which alleviates some of the pressure in the reserve market and damps the rise in the federal funds rate.

Although relatively stable for many years, the borrowing function has been less reliable recently, having gradually shifted down since the mid-1980s.

The result has been a smaller volume of adjustment credit for any given spread of the fed-eral funds rate over the discount rate. The increased reluctance to borrow at the discount window appears to be related in large part to the difficulties experienced in the banking sector during the 1980s. With large numbers of banks and thrifts failing during these years, many banks apparently became more reluctant to turn to the discount window for fear of being labeled a financially weakened insti-tution. This reluctance became acute during the economic downturn in 1990-1991, and the effec-tiveness of the discount window as a pressure release valve in the reserve market was impaired.

The instability of the borrowing function in recent years also has complicated the Federal Reserve's day-to-day operating procedures.

For part of the 1980s, the Federal Reserve relied heavily on the quantity of borrowed reserves as an "operating target" for daily reserve management. As the borrowing function became less stable, how-ever, the "borrowing target" came to be treated much more flexibly; other variables such as the federal funds rate and various measures of reserve conditions have become more important operating guides for reserve management.

SEASONAL CREDIT

The seasonal credit program was established in 1973 to assist small institutions that lack effec-tive access to national money markets and that experience a seasonal pattern of swings in deposits and loans. Previously, these banks had been forced to hold a relatively large share of their asset portfo-lio in liquid securities through much of the year to be in a position to accommodate their funding needs during the peak period of loan demand and deposit runoffs. By granting these banks longer-term funds to meet their seasonal needs, the sea-sonal credit program allows them to carry fewer liquid securities during the off-peak periods of the year and to extend more loans in their local communities. The program is structured so that larger institutions must meet a greater portion of their seasonal need through market funding sources. Typically, institutions with more than $250 million in total deposits are not able to demonstrate a seasonal need under the current structure of the seasonal program. In addition, Regulation A specifies that seasonal credit is available only if similar assistance is not available from special industry lenders.

Most lending under the seasonal credit program is to small agricultural banks in the Midwest. Agricultural banks face strong loan demand and deposit runoffs as farmers cultivate their crops dur-ing the spring and summer months. In the fall, farmers sell their crops, rebuild their deposit balances, and pay down their bank loans. Simul-taneously, banks pay down their seasonal loans with the Federal Reserve.

Banks that wish to establish a seasonal line gen-erally are required to submit three years of histori-cal data on loans and deposits to their Reserve Bank. From these data, the Reserve Bank calcu-lates the maximum amount of credit that each institution is eligible to borrow in each month of the year; the approved seasonal line also may reflect adjustments based on discussions with the borrower regarding expected funding needs in the coming year. Reserve Banks require that borrowers meet a certain portion of their seasonal need-known as the "deductible"-from their own resources. The deductible is based on the size of the borrower and reflects the presumption that larger depositories have greater access to market sources of funds and therefore should have less need for seasonal credit.

Institutions with approved seasonal credit lines are not required to exhaust all other "reasonably available" sources of liquidity before borrowing. Indeed, borrowers of seasonal credit are permitted to maintain a net "sold" federal funds position that is consistent with historical operating patterns. The Reserve Banks monitor borrowers, however, to ensure that they are using seasonal credit to fund increases in loans or deposit runoffs and that they are meeting the "deductible" portion of their sea-sonal need through their own resources. As with all forms of discount window credit, seasonal credit loans must be fully collateralized.

Usage of the seasonal credit program has grown and changed significantly over time. Since passage of the the Monetary Control Act of 1980, nonmem-ber banks have become increasingly important users of the program; indeed, in recent years, they have outnumbered member banks as borrowers of seasonal credit. Changes in the terms of the program in 1985 contributed to greater use of seasonal credit. In that year, the 4 percent deductible for the first $100 million of deposits was lowered to 2 percent, and the 7 percent deductible on additional deposits up to $200 million was lowered to 6 percent; the 10 percent deductible on deposits in excess of $200 million remained the same. These reductions were intended to help alle-viate the severe financial difficulties experienced in the farm sector during the mid-1980s.

Until recently, the rate charged on seasonal credit loans was the basic discount rate, the same rate charged for adjustment credit. The discount rate generally lies below market interest rates, and hence the seasonal program created a small subsidy for borrowers.

Given the rapid growth of sea-sonal credit over the 1980s and a judgment that financial markets had become better able to meet the seasonal funding needs of smaller banks, the Board elected to move to a market-related discount rate on seasonal credit beginning in January 1992. The market-related rate is established at the beginning of each reserve maintenance period and is based upon the average federal funds rate and the average secondary market rate on negotiable ninety-day bank certificates of deposit prevailing during the previous maintenance period.

The move to a market-related rate has not dra-matically reduced the volume of borrowing under the seasonal credit program; indeed, the peak levels of borrowing in 1994 were close to the record levels posted in 1989. In part, this continued use may indicate that borrowers still find the market-related discount rate charged on seasonal credit to be attractive relative to rates offered by their correspondents. Also important may be the nonpecuniary costs of borrowing from correspon-dents, who may impose relatively restrictive terms on the types of acceptable collateral, the size of credit limits, and the length of periods of continu-ous borrowing.

EXTENDED CREDIT

The extended credit program is designed to address the needs of institutions facing longer-term ("extended") liquidity pressures in exceptional circumstances. For the past several years, the discount rate charged on extended credit has been somewhat above market interest rates. In addition, this pro-gram affords credit only under stringent conditions. Institutions seeking extended credit must submit a business plan describing how they intend to address their liquidity difficulties, and they must have exhausted all other sources of funding before turn-ing to the window. Borrowers in the extended credit program are expected to restrain lending activity to the minimum required to remain viable in serving their markets. More generally, a bor-rower must shrink its balance sheet in an orderly manner, and its efforts to do so are closely moni-tored by its Reserve Bank. As described in detail below, the Federal Deposit Insurance Corporation Improvement Act of 1991 places restraints on dis-count window lending to institutions that do not meet minimum capital standards.

Certain borrowers drew heavily on extended credit in the 1980s, especially during the 1985-91 period, when the number of failures of banks and thrift institutions exceeded that of any period since the Great Depression.

Some of the Federal Reserve's extended credit lending in this period bridged a temporary period of illiquidity for institutions that proved to be viable, but in many other cases Federal Reserve loans were provided to institutions that were closed or required federal assistance to restore viability. Federal Reserve lending in these latter cases provided time for the FDIC and the chartering authorities to arrange for orderly closings of failing institutions. Extended credit lending was conducted in consultation with the FDIC and the relevant state and federal banking authorities to ensure that such lending would serve a clear public purpose. The Federal Reserve's lend-ing to troubled institutions during the 1980s has been the subject of some controversy, however, and a brief review of extended credit lending since 1980 provides some perspective on the Federal Reserve's actions.

EXTENDED CREDIT LENDING: 1980-85

In the late 1970s and early 1980s, the depository sector came under considerable strain as a result of a steep climb in interest rates and inflation and the ensuing deep economic recession. In the savings and loan industry, many institutions faced weak earnings on their asset portfolios at a time when their funding costs had risen sharply.

Moreover, federal limits on interest rates on deposits, in com-bination with the sharp rise in market interest rates, sparked a severe decline in deposits as account holders, in a process called disintermediation, shifted their funds into money market instruments offering higher yields. As a result, many S&Ls (as well as banks) suffered intense liquidity pressures. The Federal Home Loan Bank (FHLB) System historically had served as a key funding source for savings and loan associations by issuing debt in the national money markets and lending the proceeds to its member associations. However, by mid-1981 the magnitude of the disintermediation at thrift institutions raised the possibility that it would exceed the funding capacity of the FHLB System.

As a precautionary measure, the Federal Home Loan Banks and the Federal Reserve announced that they would lend jointly to financially sound S&Ls that needed longer-term liquidity assistance. The amount of lending under this program was relatively small; the program did, however, estab-lish a precedent for cooperation between the FHLB System and the Federal Reserve that would become important again during the S&L crisis of the late 1980s.

In another action associated with the early-1980s prospect of possibly large-scale lending to S&Ls, the Federal Reserve altered the structure of rates charged on extended credit. Since 1974, extended credit borrowers had been charged a rate of up to 2 percentage points over the basic discount rate. In August 1981, the rate structure was revised to charge the basic discount rate for the first 60 days of extended credit borrowing, the basic discount rate plus 1 percentage point for the next 90 days of borrowing, and the basic rate plus 2 percentage points for borrowing beyond 150 days. The pur-pose of the graduated rate schedule was to increase the incentive for institutions to address their liquid-ity problems as their reliance on the discount win-dow became more prolonged.

The liquidity and solvency problems among commercial banks in the early 1980s were not as severe as those in the thrift industry, but some banks were in serious trouble. In 1980, the FDIC provided extensive "open-bank assistance" to First Pennsylvania Bank, which had suffered large losses on its securities portfolio.

The Federal Reserve provided extended credit to First Pennsylvania for a time to address its liquidity needs. In July 1982, Penn Square National Bank failed owing to substantial losses on energy loans. Liquidity pressures emerged during the days immediately preceding the bank's failure, and the Federal Reserve pro-vided limited discount window assistance. Penn Square was a relatively small institution, but it was an aggressive originator of loan partici-pations. The largest single purchaser of these loan participations was Continental Illinois National Bank. Losses on loans purchased from Penn Square, coupled with other asset quality problems, led to severe liquidity pressures at Continental in early May 1984.

To address the bank's problems, staunch the outflow of funds, and prevent similar runs at Conti-nental's respondent banks, the FDIC implemented an open-bank assistance package. The FDIC also took the extraordinary step of announcing on May 17, 1984, that all general creditors of the bank would be fully protected against loss. In support of the FDIC's efforts, the Federal Reserve provided extensive discount window assistance to Continen-tal from May 1984 through September 1985.

Continental drew heavily on extended credit at a time when the highest interest rate charged for extended credit loans-2 percentage points over the basic discount rate-was lower than market rates. Concerns that Continental was obtaining sub-stantial funding at a below-market rate prompted the Federal Reserve Bank of Chicago to obtain the Federal Reserve Board's permission to apply a market-related rate to Continental's borrowing.

Later, on November 8, 1984, the Board changed the rate structure for extended credit to give all Reserve Banks the option of applying a market-related rate for extended credit borrowing beyond 150 days instead of the basic rate plus 2 percentage points. The previously established schedule of the basic rate for the first 60 days and the basic rate plus 1 percentage point for the next 90 days was left unchanged. The market-related rate was intended to apply principally to larger institutions with access to national money markets, especially during times when market rates generally exceeded the basic rate plus 2 percentage points.

EXTENDED CREDIT LENDING : 1985-90

As the problems at Continental Illinois subsided, a series of new problems began to emerge. In March 1985, a privately insured S&L in Ohio failed, rais-ing widespread concern over the safety of deposits in the numerous thrift institutions without federal deposit insurance. Soon thereafter, a liquidity crisis for privately insured institutions arose in Maryland. The Federal Reserve supplied discount window assistance in both states to help calm the situation and to permit solvent institutions to remain open. At about the same time, a severe downturn in the farm economy resulted in heavy losses for Mid-western banks in agricultural communities. And a little later, a sharp decline in oil prices led to the deterioration of portfolios of energy loans at banks in the Southwest-a situation that was soon com-pounded by a collapse in commercial real estate markets and a broad regional economic downturn.

During this period, many of the largest banks in Texas failed. With hundreds of institutions failing during the latter half of the 1980s, Federal Reserve credit was often provided to allow time for orderly resolutions, which gave depositors uninterrupted access to their funds and, more broadly, ensured that an adequate level of banking services would continue to be available.

As the frequency of extended credit lending situ-ations increased, the Federal Reserve moved to simplify its rate structure for extended credit and to broaden the use of a market-related rate. On July 27, 1987, the Board approved a policy of charging the basic discount rate for the first thirty days of borrowing and a flexible rate somewhat above market rates for borrowing beyond thirty days. The flexible rate also could be applied sooner than thirty days at the discretion of the lending Federal Reserve Bank.

By the late 1980s, the difficulties of many S&Ls far exceeded the capability of the Federal Savings and Loan Insurance Corporation to resolve them. As a result, President Bush in the early days of his administration acted to place insolvent S&Ls in federal conservatorships while the Congress devel-oped legislation to address the fundamental struc-tural, regulatory, and deposit insurance problems in the thrift industry.

To meet potential liquidity needs that might arise before legislation could be enacted, the Federal Reserve in concert with the FHLB System and the Treasury entered into a Joint Lending Program to provide liquidity to S&Ls experiencing severe withdrawals of deposits, particularly those institu-tions in federal conservatorship. Under this pro-gram, established on February 23, 1989, credit was extended only when alternative funds were not available. The Federal Reserve and the FHLB Sys-tem each advanced 45 percent of the loans, and the Treasury advanced 10 percent. Credit extensions were secured by the assets of the borrower and guaranteed by the Federal Savings and Loan Insurance Corporation.

Lending under the program was slight-only two S&Ls in conservatorship borrowed-but the program offers another example of the cooperative action of federal banking authorities to avert potential systemic crises. In August 1989, the Congress passed the Finan-cial Institutions Reform, Recovery, and Enforce-ment Act (FIRREA), which established the Reso-lution Trust Corporation (RTC) as a temporary agency charged with resolving the hundreds of S&Ls that failed. The RTC also assumed responsi-bility for any liquidity support that thrift institu-tions in conservatorship might require, so the Joint Lending Program was discontinued.

BENEFITS AND COSTS OF EXTENDED CREDIT LENDING

Concerned over the mounting frequency and cost of bank failures, the Congress in 1991 began to develop legislation to strengthen the ability of federal banking agencies to deal promptly with financially weak depositories. The Congress also undertook an assessment of Federal Reserve lend-ing to institutions whose capital had slipped below adequate levels.

The Federal Reserve had long been mindful of both the benefits and potential costs associated with prolonged lending to institutions whose solvency is unclear. An important benefit of Federal Reserve lending in these situations has been the time pro-vided to the FDIC and the other banking agencies to carry out the orderly closure and resolution of failed institutions. Arranging for the sale of a failed bank can be time consuming and labor intensive-bid documents must be prepared and potential acquirers must have time to conduct a careful review of the failed bank's assets and liabilities. This process helps the FDIC obtain the best price for the failed bank through competitive bidding by interested acquirers.

In the absence of liquidity assistance, many failed institutions would have been closed abruptly, with possible interruptions in depositors' access to their funds-including balances covered by federal deposit insurance-and in the availability of other banking services. At times of widespread financial distress, when depositors and other creditors can-not be certain of the solvency of individual banks, such disruptions may generate fears among custom-ers of other banks and thereby trigger a spread of liquidity pressures. Abrupt and disorderly closures also may adversely affect the market value of failed institutions and reduce the price obtained by the FDIC.

The Federal Reserve recognized that costs may be associated with prolonged lending to troubled institutions. Such lending, for example, can allow uninsured depositors and other general creditors to exit a failing bank before its closure. When Federal Reserve loans, which are fully col-lateralized, replace funds that are not federally in-sured, the FDIC may face higher resolution costs. In addition, a perception that discount window assistance will be readily available to troubled insti-tutions can weaken market discipline in the bank-ing system and remove some of the pressure on bank regulators to close troubled institutions promptly.

In assessing the experience of the previous years, the Congress and the Federal Reserve agreed that it would be appropriate to establish restraints on the provision of discount window credit to institutions that do not meet minimum capital standards. To this end, section 142 of the Federal Deposit Insur-ance Corporation Improvement Act of 1991 (FDICIA) sets time periods beyond which the Fed-eral Reserve may not lend to institutions below minimum capital standards without incurring a potential limited liability to the FDIC (see box, "FDICIA and the Discount Window").

Section 142 of FDICIA did not become effective until December 19, 1993. The delayed implementa-tion was intended, in part, to provide time for the federal banking agencies to exercise the new regu-latory authorities granted in FDICIA to strengthen the banking system. Nevertheless, the Federal Reserve sought to move as promptly as was pru-dent to bring its administration of the discount window into line with the provisions of sec-tion 142. The level of extended credit fell sharply (chart 4), partly reflecting a smaller number of bank failures; but the drop also reflected the more aggressive posture of the Federal Reserve and bank regulators in resolving troubled banks swiftly, which thereby reduced the need for prolonged liquidity assistance from the discount window.

POTENTIAL IMPLICATIONS OF RECENT REGULATORY DEVELOPMENTS

The panoply of regulatory changes stemming from FDICIA included many initiatives that directly link a bank's funding capability with its capital status. For example, FDICIA prohibits institutions that are undercapitalized from accepting brokered deposits. In addition, institutions that are not allowed to accept brokered deposits may also lose "pass-through" deposit insurance on new deposits or rollovers of existing deposits obtained from fidu-ciaries such as pension funds and insurance companies. Institutions that fall below minimum capital standards may face limits on the deposit interest rates they can offer to attract new deposit accounts. In addition, an undercapitalized depository may find its usual federal funds lines and respondent balances diminished as a result of a restriction, mandated by FDICIA and put in place this year, that requires banks to limit their exposure to an undercapitalized depository institution. Also, under the Federal Reserve's policies to contain payments system risk, institutions generally face tighter con-straints on their intraday reserve positions as their capital condition deteriorates.

Other regulatory developments may indirectly exert a powerful influence on bank liquidity in the future. For example, the incentive for unsecured general creditors-Eurodollar creditors and sellers of federal funds for example-to withdraw their funds at an early stage of a bank's decline is now greater because of the national depositor preference provision adopted as title III of the Omnibus Bud-get

Reconciliation Act of 1993. This provision places the claims of insured and uninsured domes-tic depositors of a failed bank ahead of the-claims of other general creditors. As a result, unsecured general creditors are at greater risk of loss in a bank failure and may flee the bank earlier to avoid such losses.

To date, strong capital and earnings for most depository institutions have mitigated the potential liquidity effects of these regulatory developments. These factors likely would become important, how-ever, in some future period of financial distress. In that event, the Federal Reserve will likely face critical decisions about curtailing the access of troubled banks to the discount window at a much earlier stage of their difficulties than was typical in the past.

8

Financial Market Crisis

THE CRISIS

Recent financial instability triggered by the collapse of the U.S. subprime mortgage market has many features with great resonance from financial history. The crisis occurred following two years of rising policy interest rates. Its causes include lax oversight and a relaxation of normal standards of prudent lending and a period of abnormally low interest rates. The default on a significant fraction of subprime mortgages has produced spillover effects around the world via the securitized mortgage derivatives into which these mortgages were bundled, to the balance sheets of hedge funds, investment banks and conduits(which are bank owned but off their balance sheets)which intermediate between mortgage and other asset backed commercial paper and long term securities. The uncertainty about the value of the securities collateralized by these mortgages spread uncertainty about the value of commercial paper collateral, and uncertainty about the soundness of loans for leveraged buyouts. All this led to the freezing up of the interbank lending market in August 2007 and substantial liquidity injections by the ECB and the Federal Reserve.

A HISTORICAL PERSPECTIVE

Many of the financial institutions and instruments caught up in the crisis are part of the centuries old phenomenon of financial innovation. The new instruments,often devised to avoid regulation, are then proved to be successful or not by the test of financial stress such as we have been recently encountering. The rise and fall of financial institutions and instruments occurs as part of a long standing pattern of booms and busts in the markets for equities, land, commodities, foreign exchange and other assets. The cycle is financed by credit. Lending booms and busts and the credit cycle are also intimately connected to the business cycle. A well known tradition in monetary economics which goes back to the nineteenth century and in the twentieth century was fostered by Wesley Mitchell (1913), Irving Fisher (1933), Hyman Minsky (1957) Charles Kindleberger (1978) and others. It tells the tale of a business cycle upswing driven by what Fisher called a displacement (an exogenous event that provides new profitable opportunities for investment) leading to an investment boom financed by bank money (and accommodative monetary policy) and by new credit instruments--financial innovation.

The boom leads to a state of euphoria where investors have difficulty distinguishing sound from unsound prospects and where fraud can be rampant. It also can lead to a bubble characterized by asset prices rising independently from their fundamentals.

The boom inevitably leads to a state of overindebtedness, when agents have insufficient cash flow to service their liabilities. In such a situation a crisis can be triggered by errors in judgement by debtors and creditors in an environment changing from monetary ease to monetary tightening. The crisis can lead to fire sales of assets, declining net worths, bankruptcies, bank failures and an ensuing recession. A key dynamic in the crisis stressed by Mishkin (1997) is information asymmetry, manifest in the spread between risky and safe securities, the consequences of which(adverse selection and moral hazard) are ignored in the boom and come into play with a vengeance in the bust.

Banks played a key role in the traditional story because bank credit in large part financed the boom, and the bust was often accompanied by bank failures and banking panics-events which inevitably made the downturn worse. This led to the traditional case for the monetary authority to act as a lender of last resort and provide liquidity at penalty rates to the money market and or discount window lending to solvent but illiquid banks.

Countercyclical monetary policy is also an integral part of the boom-bust credit cycle. My research with David Wheelock at the St. Louis Fed covering a century of U.S. data for the U.S and 9 other countries (Bordo and Wheelock 2007a and 2007b), shows that stock market booms occur in environments of low inflation, rising real GDP growth and low real policy interest rates.

As the boom progresses and inflationary pressure builds up, central banks (before World War II, driven by the gold convertibility constraint) inevitably tighten their policy rates helping to trigger the ensuing crash. The story is similar for housing booms and busts but they follow a different cyclebecause of long gestation lags in construction and in the adjustment of prices to a collapse in demand (Leamer 2007).

Stock market crashes can be serious events leading to a decline in wealth and in consumption and also a scramble for liquidity in turn contributing to incipient banking crises. Housing busts also have serious consequences for the banking system via defaults on mortgages, and on the real economy via declining wealth on consumption expenditure, the collapse of residential investment and a financial accelerator effect as net worths decline.

The recent housing boom in the U.S.was likely largely triggered by a long period of abnormally low interest rates,likely attributed to loose monetary policy from 2001 to 2004 in reaction to earlier financial turbulence and then fear of deflation and to a global savings glut (Bernanke 2007). The bust was likely induced by a rise in rates in reaction to the inevitable inflationary pressure.

The Credit Cycle

The upper panel plots,from 1953 to the present, the monthly spreads between the Baa corporate bond rate and the ten year Treasury constant maturity bond rate. The spread, inter alia, represents a measure of the financial market's assessment of credit risk and also a measure of financial instability reflecting asymmetric information (Mishkin 1991). Takes a longer view and shows the data from 1921 to the present. Also displayed in both figures are NBER recession dates and major financial market events including stock market crashes, financial crises, and some major political events that affected financial markets.

As can be seen, the peaks in the credit cycle (proxied by the spreads) are often lined up with the upper turning points in the NBER reference cycles. Also many of the events, especially the stock market crashes and the banking crises of the 1930s occur close to the peaks. Moreover the lower panel often shows the policy rate peaking very close to or before the peaks of the credit cycle. Its movements roughly reflect the tightening of policy before the bust and loosening in reaction to the oncoming recession afterwards.

The Housing Market

We next focus more closely on the housing market which is at the center of the current crisis and provide some evidence on the relationship between monetary policy, housing booms and busts and the business cycle.

The pattern suggests that housing prices tend to be procyclical and on occasion peak before the downturn, but as argued by Leamer (2007), house prices react much more sluggishly in a bust than the stock of houses as households are reluctant to cut prices. However there is somewhat of a pattern linking a tightening of monetary policy to reversals in house prices.

The Non Bank Financial Sector, Financial Innovation and Financial Crises

The traditional financial crisis story depicts a shock to a major financial or non financial firm leading to a banking panic as depositors attempt to convert their deposits into currency. More recently, especially since the advent of deposit insurance, the source of the pressure has come from the asset side, rather than the liability side of the bank's balance sheet. Examples include the Penn Central episode in 1970 when the collapse of the railroad led to a panic in the commercial paper market which led, like today, to concern by the Fed that it would spill over into the banking system.

This led the New York Fed to open the discount window to the money center banks to freely discount non financial firms based on the collateral of sound commercial paper; the Latin American debt default of 1982 when many money center banks became close to insolvent until a massive rescue was engineered between the Fed and the IMF; and the collapse of the hedge fund LTCM in 1998 which also was perceived to be a threat to the banking system. LTCM was rescued by a lifeboat operation by the New York banks orchestrated by the New York Fed. An historical precedent was a crisis in the market for bills of exchange that spread from Amsterdam to Hamburg and which like LTCM led to a liquidity crisis but in which unlike LTCM the crisis led to the failure of the principle player and many others (Schnabel and Shinn 2001). In each case the crisis broke in the non bank financial sector but spilled over or threatened to spill over onto the banks who were the ultimate creditors.

Many of the financial crises of the past involved financial innovation which increased leverage. The 1763 crisis was centered on the market for bills of exchange, Penn Central on the newly revived (in the 1960s) commercial paper market, the savings and loan crisis of the early 1980s on the junk bond market, LTCM on derivatives and hedge funds.

In the most recent episode, the financial innovation derived from the securitization of subprime mortgages and other loans has shifted risk away from the originating bank into mortgage and other asset backed securities which bundle the risk of less stellar borrowers with more creditworthy ones and which were certified by the credit rating agencies as prime. These have been absorbed by hedge funds in the US and abroad, by offshore banks and in the asset backed commercial paper of the commercial and investment banks. As Rajan (2005) argued, shifting the risk away from banks who used to have the incentives to monitor their borrowers to hedge funds and other institutions which do not, rather than reducing overall systemic risk increased it by raising the risk of a much more widespread meltdown in the event of a tail event as we are currently witnessing. As the recent crisis has demonstrated, the decline in the value of subprime mortgage paper in the US, in addition to drastically reducing the value of some hedge funds has also put pressure on the banking system which has been revealed as the ultimate creditor of the non bank financial sector.

International Spillovers

Financial crises have always had an international dimension.as Morgenstern (1959), Kindleberger (1978) and Bordo (1986) have shown. Contagion spreads quickly through asset markets, through international banking and through the monetary standard. Stock market crashes and banking panics often have occurred in many countries within a few months of the original shock. A classic example is the Baring crisis of 1890 which started in Argentina and affected the rest of Latin America and other emerging countries of the time. It was triggered by central bank tightening in England, France and Germany. This led to a series of sudden stops and current account reversals(Bordo 2006) in the emerging countries and a number of banking cries and debt defaults. These events were echoed in the late 1990s (see Calvo and Talvi 2004).

The current crisis has so far been contained to the advanced countries among which contagion has been spread by the holding of opaque subprime mortgage derivatives in diverse banks in Europe and in other countries, and by the seizing up of the asset (mortgage) backed commercial paper market. The emerging countries have so far avoided the crisis, perhaps because of the precautionary measures many have taken in reaction to their meltdowns in the Asian crisis of 1997 (e.g., the build up of large foreign exchange reserves and reduced exposure to foreign borrowing.) If the credit crunch continues and the housing bust plays out into recession in the US, then the emergers who are exposed to foreign capital will be affected as well as countries relying for their growth on exports to the US.

Policy Lessons

A number of lessons can be drawn from this historical perspective. First are the implications for crisis management and the role of the lender of last resort. The distinction made by Schwartz (1986) between real and pseudo financial crises and its extension by Bordo, Mizrach and Schwartz (1995) to systemic risk has resonance for the recent crisis events. Schwartz argued that a real financial crisis involves a scramble for high powered money by the public fearful for the safety of their bank deposits, ie a banking panic or a threat to the payments system. Pseudo crises encompass " a decline in asset prices of equity stocks, real estate, commodities;depreciation of the exchange value of a national currency;financial distress of a large non-financial firm, a large municipality, a financial industry, or sovereign debtors..." Schwartz (1986 page 12). In the case of a real crisis, the monetary authority should act as a lender of last resort and provide whatever liquidity is required to allay the public's fears. In the case of a pseudo crisis there is no need for action.

In this framework, the recent events of a collapse in the US housing market and its consequences for wealth holders directly or indirectly exposed by derivatives represents a pseudo crisis which should not be the object of central bank intervention. However the spillovers of the subprime crisis into the interbank loan market and the freezing up of liquidity to the banking system in Europe and America did pose the threat of a real financial crisis and should have been dealt with by following the strictures of Thornton (1802) and Bagehot (1873) to lend freely but at a penalty rate. Bagehot placed primary emphasis on the Bank of England lending without hesitation on the basis of collateral that would be sound in the absence of a crisis. The penalty rate was to prevent moral hazard.

The actions of the ECB of flooding the money market with liquidity and the Fed of following similar actions and also reducing the discount rate by 50 basis points in August 2007 suggests that they heeded the first part of Bagehot's lesson to lend freely on the basis of proffered collateral but not quite on the second part of lending at a penalty rate. The Bank of England until mid September 2007 followed a strict interpretation of Bagehot by keeping its discount window open to all comers but at a penalty rate.(Although the run on Northern Rock on September 14 which led to a large infusion of central bank liquidity and the announcement of a complete guarantee of all UK bank deposits very likely reflect not the failure of the Bank's LLR policy but perceived inadequacies in the UK's provision of deposit insurance, the ill thought out separation of financial supervision and regulation from the central bank and political pressure.)

The second lesson concerns the role of monetary policy in housing and other asset busts. The consensus view of monetary policy suggests that if the safety of the banking system is actually threatened by the consequences of a housing bust then the Fed should temporarily depart from its perceived mandate of maintaining price stability (implicitly targeting inflation)and provide liquidity to the financial system (Bernanke and Gertler 2001). Moreover if the collapse of housing could precipitate or exacerbate a recession then according to this view the policy to follow is countercyclical easing. As long as the Fed's commitment to its goal of a low inflation nominal anchor is perceived by market agents to be credible, such easing should not be inflationary. This seems to be the policy which the Fed by cutting the federal funds rate by fifty basis points on September 18, 2007,is pursuing.

A third lesson concerns whether the Fed should follow the reactive policy to asset booms that it now does or follow a preemptive policy. The traditional view of monetary policy argues that central banks should act reactively and deal with the consequences for the financial system of an asset price boom after it has burst (Bernanke and Gertler 2001). An alternative view argues that if an asset bubble (e.g., housing) is on the horizon, then the Fed should act preemptively to defuse it (Cecchetti 2000). Bordo and Jeanne (2002) consider a circumstance in which the use of preemptive policy against the occurrence of a low probability event, which can have catastrophic consequences, such as a national housing bust, can be welfare improving.

Finally we speculate on whether the recent financial crisis could have been avoided if the Fed had not provided as much liquidity as it did from 2001 to 2004. After Y2K when no financial crisis occurred, it promptly withdrew the massive infusion of liquidity it had provided. By contrast thereafter,it foresaw a series of shocks to the economy that might lead to financial crisis, eg the tech bust of 2001 and 9/11. In each case it injected liquidity, but when no financial crisis occurred, it permitted the additional funds it had provided to remain in the money market. In addition it overreacted to the threat of deflation in 2003-2004 which may have been of the good (productivity driven) variety rather than of the bad (recessionary) variety (Bordo and Filardo 2005). If consequent upon these events the markets had not been infused with liquidity as much as they were and for so long, then interest rates would not have been as low in recent years as they were and the housing boom which has just bust may not have expanded as much as it did. Evidence for this perspective by Taylor (2007) suggests that interest rates in this period were on average considerably lower than would be the case based on his famous rule.

THREE LIQUIDITY CRISES IN RETROSPECTIVE: IMPLICATIONS FOR CENTRAL BANKING TODAY

Liquidity problems lie at the heart of crises on financial markets as demonstrated in this paper by detailed descriptions of the stock market crash in 1987, the LTCM-crisis in 1998 and the financial market consequences of 11 September 2001. The events also demonstrate that modern central banks, in particular the U.S. Federal Reserve under Alan Greenspan, provided emergency liquidity to limit the negative effects of such crises. However, the anecdotal and empirical evidence from the three crises shows that such emergency liquidity assistance implies risks to goods price stability if it is not focused on the interbank market and quickly sterilised.

Crises have been a recurring element of the modern financial system. Liquidity problems lie at the heart of many of these crises on financial markets because market participants may not be able to sell their assets as quickly and costlessly as in more ordinary times.

This review looks at three major crises on financial markets in the United States during the chairmanship of Alan Greenspan at the Federal Reserve (Fed) from 1987 to 2006. The focus is twofold: First, I consider the role of liquidity as the (non-)ability to sell assets in the course of the stock market crash in 1987, the LTCM-crisis in 1998 and the aftermath of the terrorist attacks on 11 September 2001. This represents the microeconomic perspective of liquidity as discussed in the finance literature. Second, I examine the emergency liquidity provision by central banks, in particular by the Fed, in response to these crises. In this case, liquidity refers to a generally accepted medium of exchange or, in brief, money, which represents the macroeconomic perspective of liquidity. Since money does not need to be converted into anything else in order to make pur-chases of real goods or other assets, it is the most liquid asset and valuable in both perspectives.

The following section provides detailed descriptions of the events during each crisis. Section 3 compares the reaction of the Federal Reserve under Greenspan in response to the different crises and its implications for goods price stability. After a brief description of the model in Sauer (2007) that captures the rele-vant trade-offs of central bank interventions during liquidity crises, section 5 provides lessons from these liquidity crises for central banking in the modern market based financial system and concludes.

CHRONOLOGIES OF THE CRISES

There is a lot of empirical evidence for the role of liquidity in asset pricing.

In particular, Chordia, Sarkar and Subrahmanyam (2005) establish an empirical link between the macro-and the micro-perspective of liquidity. The authors find that 'money flows (...) account for part of the commonality in stock and bond market liquidity.' Furthermore, they use vector autoregressions to pro-vide evidence that a loose monetary policy, measured as a decrease in net bor-rowed reserves or a negative interest rate surprise, is associated with lower bid-ask spreads, i.e. increased liquidity, in times of crises.

Besides such empirical studies; there is also a lot of anecdotal evidence how central banks reacted to liquidity crises since the last decades have shown a number of such crises on financial markets. For example, Davis (1994) describes five severe liquidity crises in international markets: The Penn Central Bankruptcy in 1970, the crisis in the floating-rate notes market in the UK in 1986, the failure of the US-High Yield bond market in 1989, the Swedish Com-mercial Paper crisis in 1990 and the collapse of the ECU bond market in 1992.

Greenspan (2004) highlights three crises during his chairmanship at the Fed-eral Reserve (Fed), in which market participants wanted to convert illiquid medium to long-term assets into cash because they favoured safety and liquid-ity over uncertainty: The stock market crash in 1987, the LTCM-crisis 1998 and the terrorist attacks of 11 September 2001. This section provides a brief review of these three events and the central banks', in particular the Fed's, reactions to them.

Stock market crash in October 1987

Black Monday 1987

On 19 October 1987 ('Black Monday'), the Dow Jonex Index dropped by 22.6%. The summer 1988 issue of the Journal of Economic Perspectives provides a nice symposium of the events in October 1987. Many commentators blamed insti-tutional investors that followed a portfolio insurance investment strategy for the dramatic crash in prices. Similar to stop-loss-orders, portfolio insurance implies automatic sell orders when the value of a portfolio or single shares falls below a certain threshold.

If the absorption capacity of the market is lim-ited, portfolio insurance can cause a vicious circle of price falls and further sell orders. For example, Gammill and Marsh (1988) report official statistics that show that institutional investors who followed a portfolio insurance invest-ment strategy were the heaviest net sellers on the New York Stock Exchange and in the S&P 500 index futures market.

Furthermore, a number of traders such as arbitrageurs who traded in shares involved in takeovers or recapitalisations faced margin calls that forced them to sell shares into the falling market (Laderman, 1987, p. 28). Neely (2004, p. 32) reports enormous problems for brokerage houses and market makers as they had accumulated unusually large inventories and banks were reluctant to provide them with further credit. Garcia (1989) notes that futures, options and stock markets differed in the timing of settlement obligations, which created additional liquidity problems for investors trading off-setting positions across markets.

Grossman and Miller (1988) describe the events on 19 and 20 October against the background of their model in which market liquidity is determined by the demand and supply of 'immediacy', i.e. the willingness to trade immediately rather than to wait some time for a possibly better price. They argue that order imbalances were so great that market makers became incapable of supplying further immediacy. Market illiquidity materialised as delays in the execution and confirmation of trades and as the virtual impossibility of executing market sell orders at the quoted prices at the time of order entry.

The Fed's Response

As chairman of the Fed, Alan Greenspan managed to improve the confidence of investors and the liquidity of the market by issuing the following statement at 9 am on 20 October 1987:

The Federal Reserve, consistent with its responsibilities as the Na-tion's central bank, affirmed today its readiness to serve as a source of liquidity to support the economic and financial system (Greenspan, 1987).

The Dow Jones regained 5.9% and 10.1% on this and the following day, respec-tively. Garcia (1989) discusses the different-tools the Fed used to limit the ex-tent of the-stock market crash. These included, besides communication via the quoted statement, mainly open market operations and the use of the discount window to provide liquidity in the form of additional money to the market as well as the 'persuasion' (Bernanke, 1990, p. 148) of banks to lend freely to their customers at Wall Street. The handling of the crisis by Alan Greenspan, who had been appointed as Fed Chairman only two months earlier, laid the foundations for the belief in an insurance against stock market losses, termed 'Greenspan put' in the popular press. Taylor (2005) refers to this approach as Greenspan's 'liquidity provision principle'.

LTCM crisis in 1998

Summary

In September 1998, the near-collapse of the hedge fund Long-term Capital Management (LTCM) caused severe turmoil on financial markets.

After years of extraodinary performance, LTCM experienced below-average returns in 1997 and even losses in the first half of 1998. In response, LTCM increased its lever-age, i.e. its debt/equity ratio, and focused even more on investments in relatively illiquid assets. The Russian default in August 1998 caused a flight to quality into liquid government bonds, while the prices of more illiquid assets fell dramatically. Margin calls forced LTCM to sell its assets into the falling market, which exacerbated the crisis. Other market participants could not (and some did not want to, see Brunnermeier and Pedersen, 2005) step in and buy assets, not least because they had copied LTCM's trading strategies and were constrained in their available funds. LTCM's supposedly sophisticated risk management system had not taken this endogeneity of risk sufficiently into account and its imminent collapse threatened the functioning of the Treasury bond market because of LTCM's large short-positions on this market.

On 23 September, the New York Fed organised a private bailout of LTCM by 14 banks that had lent to the fund. In the following weeks, the Fed lowered its policy rate three times by 25 basis points in order to provide sufficient liquidity to financial markets. Both Greenspan (2004) and Meyer (2004), who was on the Fed's Board of Governors at that time, admit that the purpose of these rate cuts was to calm financial markets rather than to stimulate the still expanding real economy. Indeed, the second cut boosted financial markets and, for example, considerably lowered spreads on repos, swaps, corporate bonds and off-the-run treasuries, which all had increased dramatically after the Russian default (IMF, 1998, p. 39). Nevertheless, the Fed still feared the downside risks and lowered its policy rate a third time on 17 November despite lingering positive GDP data. Given the subsequent rise in inflation and equity prices until 2000, Meyer (2004, p. 121) later regretted this last cut.

Buildup of the Crisis

LTCM's strategy for 1998 rested mainly on a narrowing of spreads between risky bonds and safe government bonds of western industrialised countries. These spreads had widened in the course of the Asian crisis in 1997. Figure 1 shows that LTCM failed to achieve its expected annual returns of 25% already in the first months of 1998. Major losses of about 700 million U.S. $ followed in May and June as a consequence of turbulences on the market for mortgage-backed securities (MBS). In order to balance these losses, LTCM sold liquid and therefore low-yielding assets instead of dissolving illiquid positions or raising new capital. Jorion (2000, p. 288) and LTCM itself in Kolman (1999) identify this decision as a 'major' and 'critical mistake', respectively, because it made the fund even more vulnerable to margin calls on loss-generating derivative activities. In July followed the closure of Meriwether's and his colleagues' former place of work, Salomon's arbitrage trading desk in New York, due to the merger of Salomon Brothers and Travelers Group. Since this group had fol-lowed strategies similar to LTCM, the rapid liquidation of its positions caused losses for LTCM. Putman (1998, p. 46) calls this the 'proximate cause' of the imminent disaster, especially as Salomon Brothers decided to close its London arbitrage desk in September.

Eventually, on 17 August, Russia defaulted on its domestic government bonds (GKOs) and devalued its currency, taking the market by surprise as the West, lead by the IMF, had provided 22.5 billion U.S. $ a month before. This un-expected event caused a fundamental revaluation of risk premia on less liq-uid bonds and led to a flight-to-quality in liquid assets such as US or German government bonds. The associated increase of spreads sharply contradicted LTCM's expectations. The fund could not sell its positions in the market which was characterised by severe illiquidity as the significant size of the positions affected the price. After a loss of 2.5 billion U.S. $ in August alone, LTCM's survival came into question while the fund had 60,000 trading positions on its books, a balance sheet of 125 billion U.S. $ and derivatives with a notional principal amount of more than 1.4 trillion U.S. $.

The Fed's Response

When the fund tried to raise new capital to avoid bankruptcy on 2 September, it failed. After further formidable losses in September, LTCM was on the brink of bankruptcy on 21 September. Its precautionary measures against liquidity shortages, e.g. the minimum investment duration of three years or its internal risk management, had proven to be insufficient under these extreme market conditionsl. The size of LTCM as well as the significant amount of copycats of LTCM's previously successful strategies at the trading desks of many banks threatened the smooth functioning of the US treasuries market. Bill Clinton expressed the dimension of the problem when he declared that the 'world faces its biggest financial challenge in 50 years' (Economist, 1998, p. 83). Due to the threat to the whole financial system, the New York Fed under its Chairman William J. McDonough deemed it necessary to organise a private bail-out of LTCM. It arranged a consortium of 14 banks that were involved with LTCM to invest 3.625 billion U.S. $ for a 90% stake in the fund. Before that deal, Meriwether had rejected the offer of a complete takeover of LTCM by a group around Warren Buffet's Berkshire Hathaway for 250 million U.S. $ plus an in-vestment of 3.75 billion U.S. $.

The Fed lowered its target rate three times during the following weeks in order to provide sufficient liquidity to the markets. The cuts by a quarter percentage point each took place on 29 September, 15 October (between two regular meet-ings, a very rare event) and 17 November, after the target rate had stayed at 5.5% for more one and a half years. An international aid package for Brazil un-der IMF leadership further calmed the markets. After a loss of 92% in the first nine months of 1998, LTCM's portfolio regained 13% under its old manage-ment subject to the control of the banks' consortium. Its positions were com-pletely dissolved until the end of 1999 (Jorion, 2000, p. 284). Even the banks in the consortium, whose market value had suffered disproportionately during the crisis, profited strongly from the market recovery. Figure 2 includes an in-dex that summarises the market capitalisation of the banks in the consortium.

The development of the index shows not only how drastically the share prices of the consortium banks dropped during the crisis relative to the total market and the banking sector after an extraordinary performance until

July 1997, but also how quickly their market values recovered after the second interest rate cut by the Fed.

11 September 2001

Summary

The terrorist attacks in the morning of 11 September 2001 represented a very different form of a liquidity shock to financial markets. Liquidity evaporated from the financial system not because of margin calls, portfolio insurance strategies or a preference shock, but rather because large parts of the communication system and a lot of back offices in lower Manhattan were physically destroyed. One immediate response of the authorities was to leave the New York Stock Exchange, the American Stock Exchange and NASDAQ closed until 17 Sep-tember. Hence, liquidity problems concentrated in the payments and settle-ment systems and did not affect the stock market immediately. In that sense, the effects were limited and the Fed as well as the ECB could quickly withdraw the additional liquidity they had supplied to banks until 13 September within a couple of days.

Just before U.S. stock markets reopened on the morning of Monday 17 Sep-tember, the Fed cut its target rate by 50 basis points. The ECB followed suit and also lowered its key interest rates by the same amount. The Fed contin-ued to cut rates on 2 October, 6 November and 11 December, while the ECB reduced its rates only on 9 November. The contemporaneous action of central banks worldwide (see figure 4 below) on 17 September hints that this move was aimed at rebuilding confidence and signalling that central banks would con-tinue to provide liquidity if necessary. Indeed, on 17 September the Dow Jones opened only 3.2% below the closing value on 10 September. Until 21 September, the Dow lost 14.3% compared to 10 September, but regained quickly in the following weeks and reached the pre-terrorist level already in October. Hence, one can agree with Lacker (2004, p. 961) that 'the [Fed] interest rate cuts fol-lowing September 11 are probably best viewed as addressing the medium-and longer-term macroeconomic consequences' rather than a necessary response to a continuing liquidity crisis.

Financial Market Consequences of the Terrorist Attacks

The first plane hit the World Trade Center at 8:46 am local time on Tuesday, 11 September 2001, the second one at at 9:02 am. The immediate effects differed for the various financial markets mainly due to different trading times. For example, U.S. stock markets were not directly affected because trading hours at the New York Stock Exchange, the Nasdaq and the American Stock Exchange begin at 9:30 am and the authorities quickly decided not to open the equity markets and kept them closed for the rest of the week.

Other markets like the money market and the one for government bonds were severely disrupted due to the breakdown of large parts of the commu-nication system and the direct effects on several relevant market participants, in particular interdealer brokers and the Bank of New York, with offices in the World Trade Center or close-by. Lacker (2004) notes that repo trading begins at 7 am and trading in government securities at 8 am with most trading tak-ing place before 9 am. Hence, 11 September was close to a full trading day which caused severe problems for the clearing of the trades in the aftermath of the attacks. GAO (2003) reports that the number of failed transactions in the government securities markets, i.e. trades whose settlement was not com-pleted, increased dramatically, rising from around 500 million U.S. $ per day to over 450 billion U.S. $ on 12 September and staying high at about 100 billion U.S. $ daily through September 28. The same happened in the repo market and caused liquidity problems for firms that relied on this market as a fund-ing source. Overall, the physical disruptions prevented the markets from an efficient allocation of the available reserves in the financial system.

In the payments system, the Federal Reserve's Fedwire securities and pay-ments transfer systems and the private Clearing House Interbank Payments System (CHIPS) continued processing transactions but McAndrews and Potter (2002) show that Fedwire transfer volume decreased by more than 40% on 11 September and payment processing was delayed at many banks.

On Monday, 17 September, however, the transfer systems had returned to normal levels. The severest problem for the retail payments systems was the grounding of airplanes until that was only partly lifted on 13 September, which delayed the transportation and thus the clearing of checks significantly.

Central Banks' Response

On 11 September, one of the first measures of the Fed was to communicate in the spirit of the statement in October 1987 its readiness to provide liquidity to the markets:

The Federal Reserve System is open and operating. The discount window is available to meet liquidity needs.

Besides, it extended the provision of credits related to the clearing of checks, called 'floats'. Further immediate measures included substantial repurchase agreements by the New York desk of the Federal Reserve, direct lending through the discount window and swap lines to permit foreign central banks to meet liquidity needs in U.S. dollars (Neely, 2004; Lacker, 2004, see).

These interventions prevented interest rates from rising and stabilised the money market within a couple of days, as banks quickly regained confidence in the ability of other banks to meet their payment obligations.

In that sense, the effects were limited and the Fed could quickly withdraw the additional 108 billion U.S. $ in discount window credits, overnight repos and check floats it had supplied to banks until 13 September already by 20 September. Table 1 summarises the development of deposits of depository institutions with the Federal Reserve Banks from 10 September to 21 September.

Nevertheless, the money market showed significant volatility for some time as can be seen from the wide trading range of federal funds in figure 3 for almost three weeks.

In Europe, the European Central Bank (ECB) immediately issued the following press statement on 11 September:

After the unprecedented and tragic events in the United States today, the Eurosystem stands ready to support the normal functioning of the markets. In particular, the Eurosystem will provide liquidity to the markets, if need be. (ECB, 2001a)

Furthermore, the ECB conducted two one-day fine-tuning operations on 12 and 13 September with a volume of 69.3 and 40.5 billion Euro, respectively, in which all bids were satisfied.

It also entered into a swap agreement with the Fed over 50 billion U.S. $ to provide dollar liquidity to European banks on 12 September (ECB, 2001b) and thus took over the task of dollar refinancing for European banks. However, the ECB left its key interest rates unchanged on its regular meeting on 13 September.

Just before U.S. stock markets reopened on the morning of Monday 17 Septem-ber, the Fed cut its target rate by 50 basis points. The ECB followed suit and also lowered its key interest rates by the same amount.

The Fed continued to cut rates on 2 October, 6 November and 11 December, while the ECB reduced its rates only on 9 November. The contemporaneous action of central banks worldwide on 17 September hints that this move was at least partly aimed at rebuilding confidence and signalling that central banks would continue to pro-vide liquidity if necessary. Indeed, on 17 September the Dow Jones opened only 3.2% below the closing value on 10 September. Until 21 Sep-tember, the Dow lost 14.3% compared to 10 September, but regained quickly in the following weeks and reached the pre-terrorist level already in October.

The U.S. economy had been in a recession since March 2001 according to the NBER. Correspondingly, the Fed had been decreasing the funds target rate from 6.5% in the beginning of 2001 to 3.5% in August 2001 as shown in figure 5. After the fourth post-September 11 rate cut in December, the target rate remained at 1.75% for almost a year.

Given the previous development of the economy and the additional negative demand shock caused by the ter-rorist attacks on the one hand and the quick recovery of equity markets and the comparatively limited action of the ECB on the other, the extent of the rate cuts seems to be mainly driven by concerns of the Fed with respect to further macroeconomic developments in the U.S.

A COMPARISON OF THE FED'S RESPONSES

A common feature of the crises in 1987, 1998 and 2001 is that the Fed lowered its interest rate to provide emergency liquidity to the market, although the mandate of the Fed in the Humphrey-Hawkins Act of 1978 focuses on price stability and full employment.

Taylor (1993) suggested a simple interest rate Fed funds target rate with the recommendation from this Taylor rule provides a simple test for the liquidity provision principle, i.e. a temporary departure of interest rates from the Taylor rule during financial crises (Taylor, 2005) in order to avoid negative spillover effects from the asset to the goods market. The Taylor rule, however, recommended a rise of the interest rate after the crises of 1987 and 1998 as the U.S. economy showed buoyant GDP growth and rising inflation. Furthermore, the Fed had to provide liquidity for a much longer time to calm the markets in 1987 and 1998 than in 2001.

Hence, monetary policy appears expansionary for about six months until April 1988 and even more so after the LTCM-crisis 1998. In contrast, the Taylor rate matches the actual Fed funds rate after the terrorist attacks in 2001 quite closely. From the beginning of 2002, actual monetary policy looks even restrictive compared to the Taylor rule.

For comparison, inflation is measured as the annual growth rate of both the consumer price index (CPI) and the personal consump-tion expenditure index (PCE), but the differences appear to be negligible.

The average inflation rate one and a half to two years after the crises compared to average inflation in the six months up to the crises increased by 0.8 percentage points after 1987 and 1.7 points after 1998.

In contrast, inflation decreased by 0.4 (PCE) or 0.9 (CPI) points after 2001. Therefore, expansionary monetary policy via the liquidity provision principle appears to have contributed to price increases after 1987 and 1998, while a normal or even restrictive stance of mon-etary policy added to a decline of inflation after 2001.

All three historical episodes of liquidity crises demonstrate that central banks, and in particular the Fed under Alan Greenspan, stood ready to provide liq-uidity in times of financial crises.

Greenspan (2004, p. 38) states that the 'im-mediate response on the part of the central bank to such financial implosions must be to inject large quantities of liquidity,' in line with the traditional Bage-hot (1873) principle for a lender of last resort activity to 'lend freely at a high rate against good collateral.' But the events also indicate that not all financial crises are alike and central banks face a difficult task to decide on the optimal policy, which depends on the associated costs and benefits.

For example, liquidity shocks that are concentrated in the payments system allow the central bank to conduct liquidity provision in a very target-oriented manner and absorb ('sterilise') the additional liquidity quickly after the prob-lems have disappeared.

If the liquidity shock is a broader preference shock that affects financial markets in general, however, and volatility, bid-ask spreads and risk premia increase for a broad range of financial instruments, the cen-tral banks' task is more complicated: Overcoming the disruptions in the finan-cial markets and preventing fire sales requires sustained liquidity provision through interest rate decreases for some time in order to prevent fire sales of illiquid assets.

Sterilisation of this additional liquidity becomes very difficult and therefore threatens the stability of goods prices. Sauer (2007) develops a stylised model of an asset market and a goods market which provides a frame-work to analyse the relevant trade-offs for the central bank. The next section offers a brief summary of his model.

A THEORETICAL MODEL

The model in Sauer (2007) consists of two separate markets, an asset market and a goods market. The main focus is on developments on the asset market, but these developments have important implications for the goods market.

Although the monetary authority only cares about deviations of goods prices and quantities from the optimal values, the spillover effects from the asset market may require a central bank intervention on this market. In the model, investors can invest on an asset market in liquid money and potentially illiquid, but productive assets, called shares, in order to optimally satisfy their uncertain consumption needs on the goods market over two periods.

Two channels link the goods market to the asset market: First, the amount of money held by investors determines together with the size of a liquidity shock the aggregate demand of investors on the goods market which is subject to a cash-in-advance constraint.

Second, a dramatic decrease of the asset price negatively influences the goods supply in the final period because it forces in-vestors to costly liquidate their asset. Hence, the central bank faces a trade-off between inflating a demand shock today, which causes higher losses today, and limiting a negative supply shock tomorrow, which will cause higher losses to-morrow.

Expectations of central bank intervention give rise to a moral hazard effect with additional investment in less liquid, but productive shares. If the central bank has the possibility to commit to some future policy, it should optimally weight these productivity gains against the expected intervention costs.

CONCLUSION

All three historical episodes of liquidity crises demonstrate that central banks, and in particular the Fed under Alan Greenspan, stand ready to provide liq-uidity in times of financial crises.

Greenspan states that the 'im-mediate response on the part of the central bank to such financial implosions must be to inject large quantities of liquidity,' in line with the traditional Bage-hot (1873) principle for a lender of last resort activity to 'lend freely at a high rate against good collateral.' At first sight, this seems to be a simple panacea for central banks to respond to temporary liquidity crises on financial markets as central banks seem to provide liquidity at no costs. However, liquidity provision is not costless and central banking is not that simple. Depending on the nature of the liquidity shock, it may take some time until market turmoils have seized and the central bank can withdraw its liq-uidity injections.

The longer the additional liquidity circulates in the financial system, the more it will spill over into the 'real' economy, fuel goods price in-flation and thus raise the costs of the intervention. The aftermaths of the stock market crash in 1987 and the LTCM crisis in 1998 provide evidence for this mechanism, whereas the liquidity effects of the terrorist attacks on September 11, 2001, have been rather limited.

The events described in this review have highlighted a number of the relevant issues for the optimal response of monetary policy to liquidity crises. Sauer (2007) develops a model that includes the relevant trade-offs and provides fur-ther insights for optimal policy. The following questions offer a preliminary checklist that may help to determine the optimal response:

- o In which markets does liquidity dry up?
- o What causes the liquidity drain, i.e. is it really an issue of a (temporary) liquidity squeeze?
- o How large is the extent of fire sales?
- o How large are the possible spillover effects from the financial market to the rest of the economy in real (i.e. negative production effects) and nom-inal (i.e. goods price inflation) terms?

Looking at recent events in financial markets in the first half of August 2007, money market conditions were very volatile due to a number of defaults in the U.S. subprime mortgage backed securities markets that caused considerable losses for some banks. Central banks worldwide have provided substan-tial liquidity through open market operations that even exceeded the liquidity provision in September 2001 in the case of the ECB. So far, this liquidity pro-vision was intended mainly to avoid disruptions in the money market, in line with the ECB's task to promote the smooth operation of payment systems, and can be quickly sterilised.

While equity markets and other credit markets have experienced a noticeable increase in volatility and risk premia, losses have been relatively limited com-pared with the considerable increase of asset prices in recent years. If, however, the crisis dramatically spreads from the subprime market to other markets, the central banks face exactly the trade-offs described in this paper and in Sauer (2007). In particular, they should be aware of both possible spillover effects to the rest of the economy, risks to both the production and the prices of goods caused by the (non-)conduct of emergency liquidity provision.

9

Currency Crises and Capital Controls

This chapter discusses theoretical models of speculative attack and currency crises, and reviews the empirical evidence. The paper outlines the correspondence of the models to different cases of crisis (e.g. Latin American crises, the ERM breakdown, and the recent Asian crisis), and points to gaps in the theoretical literature for explaining the Asian crisis.

The large economic costs resulting from the severe depreciation of Asian currencies and general problems with macroeconomic management in the presence of large capital flows has recently led to proposals for limiting capital flows. The paper reviews the arguments and models for and against capital controls.

INTRODUCTION

The recent history of the international financial markets is characterized by numerous currency crises. Various countries around the world have come under pressure or faced a crisis at different points in time. The recent counts were the crises in Mexico in 1976 and Argentina, Brazil, Peru and Mexico in the early and mid-80s, the crises in Chile and Argentina in 1980s and ERM in 1992, then the one in Mexico in 1995. Now, in 1997 and 1998, a major part of Asia is under a financial crisis.

Economists, who are doing some catching-up work, are trying to provide analysis of these crises. So far, most of the work focuses on three different but related areas:

(a) Theoretical analysis of the causes and effects of currency crises Undoubtedly, most of the work on currency crisis focuses on explaining the causes and effects of currency crisis. Earlier work by Salant and Henderson (1978), Krugman (1979), and Flood and Garber (1984), which often are dubbed as the first-generation models, painstakingly points out how persistent government budget deficits may lead to capital flight and currency crisis. The crises in Chile and Argentina in the 1980s and ERM in 1992 led to the development of second-generation models, which emphasize the existence of multiple equilibria in the foreign exchange markets and the possibility of having crises as self-fulfilling outcomes.

The current crisis in Asia, however, has some features that either were not present or were not so obvious in previous crises. For example, these countries had responsible fiscal policies of the governments, and the economies showed solid fundamentals. Another feature of these economies is that they had been growing with impressive rates for a long period of time. Prior to the crisis, these countries were regarded by many as the model of growth for many developing countries. All of a sudden, they faced new problems in the financial markets that were not expected. It is, therefore, interesting to investigate any possible links between growth and crisis.

(b) *Empirical Studies of Crises*: On the empirical side, people have tried to determine whether crises can be predicted. In particular, there has been interest on finding the relationship between a crisis and certain variables of the economy, and whether there exist good leading indicators of a crisis.

(c) *Policy Recommendation*: As the analysis of various crises is being developed, a question that easily pops up in people's mind is what the government should do to avoid a crisis. Two approaches can be suggested. First, one can focus on a particular crisis, determine its causes, and try to see whether some of these causes can be eliminated through a change in some government policies. For example, if one looks at the crises in Latin America, one can simply suggest that lowering the government deficits could avoid a crisis down the road. Second, one can examine the similarities between various crises and determine whether there are some government policies that could diminish the chances of a crisis in the future. In terms of the second approach, one can note that while all crises can be distinguished in terms of their causes and effects, they do share two common features: (i) a fixed exchange rate regime, and (ii) capital flight and speculative attacks. Corresponding to these two features, two proposal have been suggested: (i) give up the fixed exchange rate regime; (ii) capital control, i.e., strict constraints on the inflow and/or outflow of capital across the borders of a country.

In this paper, we survey some of the more important issues related to currency crises. Our discussion will be based the three areas described above: the analysis of causes and effects of crises, empirical studies, and policy recommendation.

In analyzing the causes and effects of crises, we begin with the two main areas emphasized in earlier work: the existence of persistent fiscal deficits, and existence of multiple equilibria and self-fulfilling crises.

We then turn to more recent work that examines other areas: (a) simultaneous existence of a banking crisis and a currency crisis, so called the twin crises; (b) herd behavior and its relationship to capital flight and speculative attacks; and (c) moral hazard and currency crises.

We will not mention about the other policy suggestion: the floating of a local currency. It is because a fixed exchange rate versus a flexible exchange rate has long been an important issue in the literature, and we decided not to cover this area.

For an economy under a fixed exchange rate regime, a currency crisis usually refers to a situation in which the economy is under the pressure to give up either the prevailing exchange rate or the regime. For the former, the economy in crisis in most cases is required to devalue its currency by a substantial amount, and the exchange rate then moves to a new, but at least temporarily fixed, level. For the latter, the alternative regime is a flexible exchange rate one.

In the literature, many models and theories have been suggested to explain the causes and occurrence of a currency crisis. In this section, we focus on the impacts of domestic credit creation on the exchange rate pegged by the government. Models that use these impacts to explain the existence of a currency crisis are sometimes called the first-generation models.

A Simple Model of Exchange Rate Determination

To introduce the main features of the first-generation models, let us first lay down a simple model of exchange rate determination. Consider a one-sector, small, open economy. To focus on the monetary side of the economy, we assume that its real side is characterized by full employment, with constant factor endowment and technology. The following equilibrium conditions are used to describe the monetary side of the economy:

(1) tttbiaP/M

(2) ttttDRSM

(3) tttS*PP

(4) tttS*ii

where tM, tP, ti, are the quantity of (high-powered) money, the general price level, and the interest rate, respectively. Equation (1) is the money demand equation, with the output level always at a fixed level. The two coefficients, a and b, are positive numbers. Equation (2) gives the money supply, which consists of foreign reserves (in foreign currency) held by the government/central bank, tR, plus domestic credit, tD. Variable tS is the spot exchange rate, defined as the domestic currency price of foreign currency. Equation (3) is the purchasing power parity, where an asterisk represents a foreign variable, while equation (4) is the interest parity condition, where a dot above a variable represents the rate of change of that variable with respect to time. Assuming perfect foresight, expected rate of depreciation is equal to the actual rate of depreciation. Since we are considering a small economy, foreign variables are treated as given exogenously.

This allows us to normalize 1*Pt and 0*it.

In this subsection, we assume that the spot exchange rate always adjusts to its equilibrium level instantaneously and costlessly. With no government intervention, the amount of foreign reserve is fixed and is denoted by 0R.

The domestic credit is assumed to be increasing at an exogenously given rate of 0, i.e., tD. The increase in domestic credit is the main feature of most currency crisis models. Several reasons can be used to explain why it increases, but the most common one is that the government is running continuous deficits, and that these deficits are financed by printing money (increase in domestic credit).

Combining equations (1), (3) and (4) together, we have (5) tttSbaSM. The solution to equation (5) can be found to be (6) ttMS, where 2/a b and a/1.

Recall that the high-powered money consists of foreign reserves and domestic credit, (2) can be substituted into (6) to give (7) ttDS, where)R/(011. Equation (7) is represented by line ABCE in Figure 1. The vertical intercept of the line, A, represents)1/(0R.

Suppose that initially at time 0tt, the quantity of domestic credit is 0D. This is represented by point B. As the domestic credit increases, the currency is devalued and the exchange rate moves up along the line BCE. Note that because of the constant rate of increase in tD, can be interpreted as a diagram showing the change in tS with respect to time, with t represented by the horizontal axis. Because tD is changing at a rate of, the value of tD at time t is)tt(DDt00. Using this equation, the exchange rate will change according to the following equation: (8))tt(DSt00.

Note that the exchange rate given in (8) depends on the initial value of foreign reserve. We can consider an alternative rate that corresponds to another reserve level, conve-niently chosen to be zero, 00R. This implies that. Denote the corresponding rate by tS, which is described by (9))tt(DSt00. The exchange rate in (9) is represented by line GHJ.

Suppose now that at time 0tt, in an unanticipated move, the government chooses to raise the exchange rate from the prevailing level to a higher level. In Figure 1, this policy can be represented by a jump of the exchange rate from point B to F instantaneously. After the jump, the exchange rate is then fixed, as represented by horizontal line S FC.

When the exchange rate is fixed, 0tS. Equation (4) implies that i = i* = 0, so that equation (1) reduces to (9) SaMt, i.e., the equilibrium stock of money is proportional to the given exchange rate. Therefore when the government pegs the exchange rate, the economy accumulates foreign reserve and thus money by running a balance of payment surplus.

Domestic Credit Creation and Currency Crisis

Mexico in 1976, and Argentina, Brazil, Peru and Mexico in the early and mid-80s experienced various degrees of currency crises. These countries chose to peg their currencies against foreign ones. At some points they observed capital flight and speculative attacks on their currencies, which resulted in enormous pressure on the central bank to devalue their currencies.

Continuous government fiscal deficits had been attributed as one major factor of these currency crises. These deficits were financed mainly by printing money, i.e., through an increase in the domestic credit held by the central banks. As Salant and Henderson (1978), Krugman (1979), and Flood and Garber (1984) pointed out, there is an inconsistency between deficit financing policy and the policy of a fixed exchange rate. In the model described above, the money supply that equilibrates the money market is given exogenously.

An increase in the central bank's domestic credit will be matched by a drop in foreign reserve. Because the amount of foreign reserve held by the central bank is finite, the government cannot maintain a fixed exchange rate regime indefinitely. Krugman went on to argue that a crisis occurs when the central bank's foreign reserve reaches a minimum level. At this point, the government will have to devalue its currency or give up its fixed exchange rate policy. Let us make use of the simple model of exchange rate introduced earlier to explain such an inconsistency.

Let us assume that at some point, the economy is represented by point F, with the exchange rate fixed at S, while domestic credit is increasing at a rate of. The increase in domestic credit means that point F shifts to the right along the horizontal line. However, by equation (9), the equilibrium money stock is fixed, meaning that as the economy is creating domestic credit, it is losing foreign reserve by running balance of payment deficits. In other words, because 0tM, we have (10) 0S/S/DRtt. Equation (10) suggests that the amount of foreign reserve at any time t is given by (11))tt(RRt00, where S/.

If this situation continues, the central bank will run out of foreign reserve at time xtt, where xt is obtained from (11) by setting 0tR: (12)./Rttx00 At xtt, the value of domestic credit is (13) 0000RSD)tt(DDxx. As more domestic credit is created, both flexible exchange rates tS (with positive foreign reserve) and tS (with no foreign reserve) are rising. Specifically, SSt when ytt,where from (8), (14))DS(tty00. Similarly, SSt when yzttt, where (with1)(15))DS(ttz00. It is usually assumed that xytt.

The value of domestic credit at ytt is equal to (15))S(D)()tt(DDyy0001, and that at ztt is equal to (16))()1()(000SDttDDzz.

Obviously, because the amount of foreign reserve held by the central bank is limited, the present situation cannot continue indefinitely. Suppose that the government decides that this situation terminates when foreign reserve hits a minimum level such as zero, and that it gives up its fixed exchange rate policy and lets the currency float.

When the constraint is removed, the exchange rate becomes the same as the shadow rate. Such a reversal of the exchange rate policy is a crisis for the economy under consideration because the government is forced to abandon its originally set exchange rate policy, after losing a considerable amount of foreign reserve. Krugman (1979) points out that the fixed exchange rate regime can no longer survive when the amount of foreign reserve held by the central bank reaches a minimum level.

Flood and Garber (1984), however, argue that if people know in advance of the devaluation, speculation will occur and could force the devaluation to happen earlier. For example, shortly before xt, speculators can purchase from the central bank the remaining foreign reserve, denoted as

'R; with an amount of domestic currency of 'RS. When the exchange rate is changed to S'S, where 'S is the corresponding shadow exchange rate, the speculators can sell the foreign reserve back to the central bank, and get a profit of 'R)S'S(. This profit may not be much if 'R is small, but the profit rate is very high considering the short duration of time. So devaluation will not occur at xtt, but earlier. However, the same argument can be used to say that devaluation will not occur just earlier than xt, but even earlier. As a result, at any time when the shadow exchange rate is higher than the pegged rate, one can argue that devaluation will occur slightly earlier. This means that the crisis will occur when ztt, and the change in central bank's foreign reserve over time is described by ABE in Figure 2. Furthermore, the above analysis implies that there is no discrete jump in the exchange rate.

However, the path ABE of foreign reserve requires perfect information, costless exchange transactions, unlimited resources owned by the speculators, and a clear policy in terms of when the fixed exchange rate is given up. It should also be pointed out that between yt and zt, the currency is overvalued (relatively to the existing stock of foreign reserve held by the central bank).

Therefore, if the determination of the government in defending the pegged exchange rate is unknown to the public and people do not know the minimum amount of foreign reserve below which the government will give up the exchange rate regime, then it is possible that some investors may start moving the money out of the country at or shortly after yt. These may be people who are most pessimistic about the economy or the resolve of the government. This leads to loss of foreign reserve of the government, making devaluation more likely. Very soon, more people may take similar action, and speculative attack occurs. Finally, the capital flight and speculation become so overwhelming for the government to defend the exchange rate anymore.

Speculative Expectations, Multiple Equilibria, and Self-fulfilling Crises

While the model of currency crisis presented in the previous subsection shows the inconsistency between continuous creation of domestic credit and a fixed exchange rate, it has been pointed out that a currency crisis can also occur without the financing of fiscal deficit through domestic credit creation. The crisis that appeared to be stranger is the experiences of certain European countries in 1992-1993. In this period, while maintaining fixed exchange rates, these countries faced severe speculative attacks on their currencies.

In August 1993 member countries of the European Monetary System gave in and allowed more flexibility in their currencies, permitting their currencies to move within a band of 15 percent instead of 2.25 percent for most Exchange Rate Mechanism (ERM) rates. However, it is interesting to note that two years later the prices of some of these currencies were at about the level same as before. This means that these European countries were not having any obvious macroeconomic troubles and that currency crises can arise even when economies have sound macroeconomic fundamentals. In other words, these countries do not have the features that are described by the first-generation models.

Looking at the breakdown of the ERM, Obstfeld (1994) suggests the following features of the type of crises experienced by these European countries:

1. There are reasons why the government wants to abandon the peg (to inflate away the debt burden denominated in domestic currency, and to follow expansionary monetary policies in case of unemployment, etc)
2. There are reasons why the government wants to defend the peg, hence a conflict between the two (to

facilitate international trade and investment, to gain credibility if has a history of high inflation, and as a source of national pride or commitment to an international cooperation).

3. The cost of defending the peg rises when people expect the peg would be abandoned, because people in the past expected that the exchange rate would be depreciated now.

Hence, anticipation of devaluation makes the debt-holders and worker unions in the past demand higher interest rate and wages, making debt-burden too high and industries un-competitive at the current exchange rate level. The important trigger is the expectation of people. If they expect that the currency is going to be devalued in the near future, they could expect enormous pressure on the central bank even though the conditions of the economy are solid. Such expectations may lead them to convert their domestic currency to foreign currency before the devaluation. If sufficient number of people do that with large sums of domestic currency, the central bank could run out of foreign reserve and has to devalue the currency. In this case, the crisis is self-fulfilling. Sometimes the models that emphasize the above characteristics are called the second-generation models.

However, Krugman (1998a) supposes that a fixed exchange rate could be costly to defend, if people now expect that it will be depreciated in the future. The usual channel involves short-term interest rates: to defend the currency in the face of expectations of future expectations may either worsen the cash flow of the government (or indebted enterprises) or depress output and employment. The model introduced earlier can be used to explain the feature of a self-fulfilling currency crisis. Suppose that the central bank currently owns foreign reserve 00R, and that the government is keeping the domestic credit constant, 0. From (7), with 0, the flexible exchange rate corresponding to a foreign reserve of 0R is given by (17) ttDS, which is illustrated by line OAB in Figure 3.

Let the current domestic credit be AD, and let the exchange rate be pegged at S. This is depicted by point A in the diagram. Since the domestic credit is fixed, the economy can avoid the type of crisis as described above, and can stay at point A indefinitely. Suppose now that currency speculators believe that there is a positive probability that the government will devalue the currency in the near future. Specifically, suppose that the government will let the currency go if the foreign reserve runs down to a minimum level, such as zero, and that the shadow exchange rate will then be equal to the flexible rate.

If the speculators have the resources and choose to purchase all the foreign reserve held by the central bank, the government will give up its fixed exchange rate policy, and the exchange rate will jump up to SS 1, as represented by point F. Such devaluation occurs despite the fact that the economy is fundamentally solid, with no domestic credit creation due to deficit financing. In terms of the resources held by the speculators, Obstfeld (1996) distinguishes among three different cases: (a) when the total resources of the speculators are less than 0R ; (b) when the resource of each speculator are greater than 0R ; (c) when none of the speculators has resources greater than 0R, but when two or more of them combined will have resources greater than 0R. In case (a), devaluation will not occur. In case (b), devaluation will occur when any one of the speculators purchases 0R from the central bank, causing devaluation. In fact, all of them will try to be the first to do so. In case (c), if sufficient number of speculators believe that devaluation will occur and they rush to purchase foreign reserve, devaluation will definitely occur, even though without speculation the fixed exchange rate regime could have survived indefinitely. If the currency is devalued, the total profit of the speculators is 01)(RSS. The crisis that occurs in case (c) has two features: (1) there are multiple equilibria. (2) It is self-fulfilling in the sense that it will not occur if none of the speculators act, but will occur if a sufficient number of them act. Figure 3 also shows that a self-fulfilling crisis can occur when domestic credit is in between AD and ED. As explained before, if the central bank loses all its foreign reserve, the exchange rate becomes flexible, jumping up to a point in between E and F on CEFG. If the initial value of domestic credit is equal to ED, the speculators will earn no profit.

If the initial domestic credit is less than ED, no speculation will occur because if the fixed exchange rate breaks down, appreciation of the currency will occur and the speculators lose money. If domestic credit is greater than AD, the currency is overvalued. The speculators will have a bigger incentive to attack the exchange rate. There are some models in which the objectives of the government are spelled out, and multiple equilibria are derived explicitly.

TWIN CRISES: BANKING AND EXCHANGE RATE CRISES

The new generation models emphasize the importance of financial sector and capital flows in currency crises. Hence, the term "twin crises". The frequent occurrence of twin crises (Nordic countries in 1990s, Turkey in 1994, Venezuela, Argentina and Mexico in 1994, Bulgaria in 1996, and Asian countries in 1997) has been a result of banking crisis precipitating a currency crisis, either by an increase in money supply, or by a large scale withdrawal leading to a decrease in money demand. The causation between the balance of payments and banking crises is, however, debatable. Stoker (1995) and Mishkin (1996) argue that balance of payments crisis leads to banking crisis. According to Stoker, an external shock, coupled with commitment to fixed exchange rate, leads to loss of reserves. If this loss of reserves is not sterilized, then a speculative attack is followed by a period of abnormally high interest rates leading to credit crunch, increased bankruptcies and financial crisis. Mishkin argues that devaluation could weaken the position of the banks if they have a large share of their liabilities denominated in foreign currency.

However, Diaz-Alejandro (1985), Velasco (1987), Calvo (1995) and Miller (1995) argue that banking crises lead to balance of payments crises. The argument is that central banks bailout financial institutions by printing money, and this erodes their ability to maintain the prevailing exchange rate commitment. But Reinhart and Vegh (1996) suggest that the two crises have some common causes-an example of "perverse" dynamics of an exchange rate based inflation stabilization plan. Since prices are slow to converge to international levels, exchange rate appreciates markedly. Initially, there is a boom in imports and economic activity, which is financed by borrowing abroad. This leads to a widening of current account deficits and financial markets infer that stabilization program is unsustainable, hence the currency is attacked. The increase in bank credit during the boom is financed by foreign borrowings, when capital flows out and asset market crashes, it leads to the collapse of the banking system as well.

McKinnon and Pill (1996) show that financial liberalization along with some microeconomic distortions-like implicit insurance deposits-can make boom-bust cycles more pronounced as they lead to lending boom that leads to the eventual collapse of banking system. Goldfajn and Valdes (1997) show that changes in international interest rates and capital inflows are amplified by the intermediating role of banks and how these swings may produce business cycles that ends in bank runs and financial and currency crashes.

However, the stylized facts that these models tend to explain are: (Goldfajn and Valdes, 1997 and Kaminsky and Reinhart, 1996)

1. Banking crises are highly correlated to currency crises.
2. Capital inflows increase steadily before the crisis and fall sharply during the crisis.
3. Banking activity (intermediation) increases some time before the collapse.

Goldfajn and Valdes (1997) model the interaction of liquidity creation by financial intermediaries with capital flows and exchange rate collapses in a two time-period framework, hence focussing on the role of the financial intermediaries in the currency crises. These intermediaries provide liquidity, which is attractive to foreign investors with short-term incentives for investment, hence helping in capital inflows. However, due to any exogenous shocks, when the foreign investors want to withdraw their deposits, these intermediaries, being locked in illiquid assets, face the risk of failure. Hence, a bank run leads to capital outflows and currency collapse. Their model provides role for the banking system in magnifying the shocks to fundamentals (productivity and interest rates), but does not assume any kind of inconsistency in policy making, like the first and second generation models.

Some of the important results from their model are:

1. Under intermediation, the probability of a run will be positive and non-decreasing with respect to international interest rate.
2. There are proportionally more capital outflows with intermediaries in period 1.
3. There is a trade-off in the sense that intermediation may generate larger inflows, but, at the same time, a higher probability of a run against the country.
4. If devaluations are expected, runs against the intermediary are more likely.

5. The intermediation process generates a transmission and amplification mechanism in which small shocks translate into larger effects.

HERDING AND CAPITAL FLIGHT

In this section, we turn to another explanation of the existence of currency crisis: herd behavior. Herding, which is an example of information cascade, is said to exist when individuals tend to choose actions similar to previous actions chosen by other individuals. In other words, with herding effects, individuals tend to move in conformity, and a small shock to society could lead to a mass shift in the actions of people. In some special cases, people can choose to give up the private information or signals they possess and follow the actions of others, even though the private information or signals they have would suggest them to act otherwise.

A famous example is Keynes' beauty contest example.

Earlier work includes the papers by Leibenstein (1950) on the bandwagon effects. Recently, more rigorous models have been suggested to explain herd behavior.

Several models that have been introduced to explain investment behavior are mentioned here.

Froot, et al (1992) show that speculators with short horizons may herd on the same information, trying to learn what the other informed traders know. These could lead to multiple equilibria, and herding speculators may even choose to study information that is completely unrelated to fundamentals. So, the large perceived penalty for missing a bull market leads managers to follow the pack even if fundamentals do not warrant it; conversely, the penalty of losses during the bear market are lower as all other managers are losing money as well.

Krugman (1998a) suggests similar reasons why herding might occur. First, there is a bandwagon effect, which is driven by the awareness that investors have private information-where investors ignore their own information and thrive on the information of other investors. It has been argued that bandwagon effects in markets with private information create a sort of "hot money" that at least sometimes causes foreign exchange markets to overreact to news about national economic prospects. Second, much of the money invested in crisis-prone countries is managed by agents rather than directly by principals-where the principal-agent problems arise.

The above models usually assume sequential actions by individuals, so that those who take actions later will observe what actions others have taken previously. Calvo and Mendoza (1998) introduce a model in which herding can exist even when individuals have simultaneous decision making. They find that with informational frictions, herding behavior may become more prevalent as the world capital market grows. With globalization, the cost of collecting country-specific information to discredit rumors increases and managers, facing reputational costs, choose to mimic the market portfolio. Hence, small rumors can induce herding behavior and move the economy from a no attack to an attack equilibrium.

Herding is a type of distortion in the economy in the sense that the actions of some individuals can produce externality. This has two implications, both are important in explaining the occurrence of a crisis. First, the actions of a limited number of individuals may produce at best some limiting adverse effect on an economy. The same action of a large number of individuals can make a possible damage unbearable. For example, Obstfeld (1996) argues that in some cases, the attacks by a limited number of speculators on the local currency will not do much harm, as the central bank has enough foreign reserves to defend. However, if a large number of speculators launch similar attacks, the central bank could run out of reserve and the country could face a crisis. Another example is the current crisis in Asia.

For countries like Thailand or South Korea, failure of firms in the economy is nothing strange, and as long as the number of failures during any period of time is limited, the economy usually has capacity to absorb these losses. However, if widespread failures exist at about the same time, huge bad loans can be created, and financial institutions could face repayment problems if the money originally comes from abroad.

Furthermore, if the values of bad loans were not high, these financial institutions can borrow more to ease the cash flow problem, but if the bad loans are high, it is difficult to borrow such large amounts in a short time. Another externality created by herding is that while certain massive actions may hurt the economy, these actions could be entirely rational from individuals' point of view.

Such rational behaviors occur when there are payoff externalities (payoffs to an agent adopting an action increases as the number of agents adopting that action increases) or principal-agent problems (managers have an incentive to hide in the herd so that their actions cannot be evaluated).

Of course, as Flood and Marion (1998) argue, in many cases, herding could explain some part of the currency crises in Asia, but not the whole. First, individuals are less likely to ignore their own or new information in a world where they can adjust their strategies continuously to new information. Second, in case strategic interactions are important, then the cascade story is unsatisfactory, because the potential capital gains arising from the action of one agent does not depend on actions chosen by others.

Wong (1998) applies herding behavior to provide a theory of the formation of bubbles in the housing market in case of Thailand, and explains how the bubbles had caused some of the troubles in the economy. When the growth of the economy creates rising demand of housing, investors respond with more supply. Consecutive periods of high growth reward the more optimistic and aggressive investors with huge profits. These profits and successes prompt pessimistic investors to revise upward their beliefs of the future and become more aggressive. More firms enter the market and ride the bandwagon. Bubbles are then formed when (a) investors get too optimistic; or (b) a widespread failure and bankruptcy of firms in the housing market creates big losses to financial institutions, which in turn could not repay their foreign debts; or (c) a widespread failure and bankruptcy of firms in the housing market creates pessimism and panics in the economy, prompting capital flight and speculative attacks on the domestic currency.

MORAL HAZARD AND FINANCIAL CRISES

Moral hazard can occur under asymmetric information because borrowers can alter their behavior after the transaction has taken place in ways that the lender regards as undesirable. In financial markets, however, moral hazard could occur in the absence of asymmetric information; i.e., moral hazard arises from the possibility that investor behavior will be altered by the extension of government guaranteed that relieve investors of some of the consequences of risk taking.

Krugman (1998b) and Corsetti, et al (1998) have proposed moral hazard as a possible explanation for currency crises, especially the Asian crisis of 1997. Krugman considers a case of over-guaranteed and under-regulated financial intermediaries. Since these institutions do not have to put any capital up-front, and have the liberty to walk away at no personal cost in case of bankruptcy, the economy engages in excessive investment. This economy is made worse off by globalization. If it did not have access to world capital market, then excessive investment demand by these intermediaries would show up as high rates of interest, and not as excessive investment. But access to world market allows the moral hazard in the financial sector to translate into real excess capital accumulation.

Cōrsetti, et al (1998) also recognize moral hažard as a source of over-investment, excessive external borrowing and current account deficits. Unprofitable projects and cash shortfalls are re-financed through external borrowing as long as foreign creditors lend to domestic agents against future bail-out revenue from the government. The government deficits need not be high before the crisis, but refusal of foreign creditors to re-finance the debt forces the government to step in and guarantee the outstanding stock of external liabilities. The government might recourse to seigniorage revenues. Expectations of inflationary financing thus cause a collapse of the currency and anticipate the event of a financial crisis.

In fact, the argument of moral hazard is not only applicable to the intermediaries, but also to the governments. Proponents of moral hazard argue that IMF creates bailout for the governments or investors in the event of a crisis. However, Radelet and Sachs (1998) do not see the current Asian crisis as a result of carelessness on the part of the investors because they were sure to be bailed out in a crisis. First of all, only state-owned enterprises can be bailed out in a crisis. According to Radelet and Sachs, if the creditors feared a risk of a crisis in Asia, then spread on Asian bonds should have increased, but it did not. If the creditors felt an increasing risk of government-led bailout, then ratings of long term government bonds should have gone down, but they did not either. A large part of the investment went into the risky equity market, and bank loans went to non-financial corporate sector, where the direct government bailout was least possible. Creditors have been aware of weak bankruptcy laws and ineffective judicial systems in Asia. Hence, the foreign investors lent because they anticipated these economies to perform well, and not because they believed that they would be bailed out.

PREDICTABILITY OF CRISES

There are different definitions of crisis that have been used in empirical literature. Some papers use a narrow definition of crisis as a devaluation of exchange rate. Other papers use the term crisis in a broader sense, i.e., as an increase in Market Pressure Index(MPI). It is constructed as follows: where e is the bilateral exchange rate of country "i" with US or Germany; i is the interest rate in country "i" and r is the non-gold international reserves that the central bank has; the changes in exchange rate, interest rate and reserves are weighted by their respective standard deviations. This index is high when there is pressure on the currency and low otherwise. The intuition is that if there is an attack on the currency, either the exchange rate would depreciate, or interest rate would be raised to ward off the attack, or the central bank would sell foreign currency to support the exchange rate. Most papers use probit or logit analysis, where the dependent variable is a discrete measure of crisis, which is also the probability of a crisis. For example, Eichengreen, Rose and Wyplosz (1996a) define the dependent variable as:

DUMMPIx = 1 if MPIx > MPIx + 1.5* MPIx, , 0 otherwise; where is the mean of the MPI in country x, and is the standard deviation of MPI.

Kaminsky and Reinhart (1996) construct the MPI as a weighted average of exchange rate changes and reserve changes, and define crisis as:

DUMMPIx if MPIx MPIx MPIx 130 otherwise *,

The exclusion of incidents of speculative pressure on the exchange rate below the arbitrary threshold value has the disadvantage of introducing sample bias into the estimation procedure. Flood and Marion (1998) argue that many models of speculative attack indicate that unanticipated devaluations produce the largest jump in the MPI. The size of jumps in the MPI at the time of attack is reduced by the extent to which the attack is anticipated. Thus, selection of only extreme values of the MPI (as in construction of the dependent variable for probit models) may reduce the share of predictable crises in the sample and reduce the number of crises that are likely to be correlated with fundamental economic determinants. Cerra and Saxena (1998) use Markov Switching Models (MSMs), which make the probability of a crisis continuous and endogenous. Radelet and Sachs(1998b) define a financial crisis as a sharp shift from capital inflow to capital outflow between year t-1 and year t.

A banking crisis could be defined in either of the two ways: financial distress meaning a situation of insolvency of banks, or financial panic referring to illiquidity in the banking sector. A run on the bank occurs when individual depositors withdraw money from the bank because they fear that "other depositors" are withdrawing money, and not because banks have made bad investments. This immediate withdrawal of funds by all depositors makes the banks illiquid, and the bank run a success.

Kaminsky, Lizondo and Reinhart (1997), Kaminsky and Reinhart (1996) and Kaminsky (1998) use the signals approach, where the idea is that economy behaves differently during crisis and tranquil times. The events that start a crisis will be present in "the leading indicators" before the actual crises and thus will help currency crises. This approach involves monitoring the evolution of a number of economic variables to find whether the variables are behaving in an anomalous way and thus are "signaling" a future crisis. This approach involves specifying a "threshold", beyond which the variable sends a "signal" of future crisis-the signal could be an accurate one or give a "false alarm". The 24-month before the crisis erupts is defined as "crisis" times, while the rest of the months are defined as "tranquil" times. The choice of threshold determination involves striking a balance between Type I (Rejecting H0 when H0 is true) and Type II (Accepting H0 when H0 is false) errors. The sizes of the errors are and, respectively. If is 0 (the threshold is too lax), then the indicator will catch all the crises, but will give lots of false signals (noise). If is 0 (the threshold is too tight), the indicator will never issue a false signal, but it will miss all the crises. Hence, for each variable, the critical region is selected so as to minimize the noise-to-signal ratio:

Noise-to-signal ratio = 1

where () 1 number of months with good signals number of months in the crisis window number of months with bad signals number of months outside the crisis window where goods signals are the signals inside the crisis window and bad signals are the signals that are outside the crisis window, and the crisis window is the 24-months preceding the crises.

The most common leading indicators used in the literature are:

1. Over-borrowing cycles: M2 multiplier, domestic credit/ GDP, financial liberalization;
2. Bank runs: Bank deposits;
3. Monetary Policy: "excess" M1 balances;
4. Balance of Payments problems: exports, imports, terms of trade, real exchange rate, reserves, M2/ reserves, real interest rate differential, world real interest rate, foreign debt, capital flight (deposits of domestic residents in BIS banks) and short-term foreign debt/total foreign debt;
5. Growth slowdown: output, domestic real interest rate, lending /deposit rate ratio, stock prices.

The following shocks signal vulnerability to a crisis:

1. Since crises are preceded by over-lending cycles, signals are associated with large positive shocks to the M2 multiplier, the domestic credit /GDP ratio,

excess real M1 balances, and M2/reserves, and high levels of foreign debt.

2. Problems in the capital account can worsen if foreign debt is concentrated at short maturities and there is capital flight. So large positive shocks to these indicators are associated with possible future crises.
3. Large positive shocks to the lending/deposit interest rate ratio and to real interest rates are taken as signals of crises.
4. Large negative shocks to deposits warn of future financial fragility.
5. The weak external sector is captured by large negative shocks to exports, the terms of trade, the real exchange rate and reserves and large positive shocks to imports, the real interest rate differential, and the world real interest rate.
6. The recessions are captured by large negative shocks to output and to the stock market.

CAPITAL CONTROL: A REMEDY?

The current crisis in Asia has renewed an old debate on whether a country, especially the emerging economies like Thailand, Malaysia, and Indonesia, should limit the inflow and outflow of capital as its economy is growing. People are alarmed by the size of the speculative attacks on local currencies of these countries and the possible damages caused by a sudden outflow of capital on the central bank's foreign reserve stock and the financial and real sides of the economy.

All these countries, after months of attacks on their currencies and massive depletion of the reserve stocks, eventually gave up their fixed exchange rate regimes. In the nineties, while these countries were growing impressively, they attracted large amounts of capital from investors all over the world. In 1997, as the prospect of devaluation became more and more likely, everyone tried to move his/her capital out of these countries as soon as possible. That created a huge swing in the direction of movement of capital. While in 1996, the 5-Asian economies (South Korea, Indonesia, Malaysia, Thailand and the Philippines) received net private capital inflows amounting to $93billion, in 1997, they experienced an estimated outflow of $12.1billion, a turnaround in a single year of $105billion, amounting to more than 10% combined GDP of these economies (Rodrik 1998).

The ease of capital movement across the borders of the countries, which was at a time regarded as the main reason for attracting capital which is used for domestic investment and growth, allowed foreign investors to move their capital out in 1997, and facilitated speculative attacks. It was therefore straightforward to blame these currency speculators and question the wisdom of allowing capital movement in the first place. In fact, Malaysia was the first country in the current crisis (and the only one so far) to turn to a strict control on inflow and outflow of capital.

In the following sections, we will present several issues about capital control and arguments for and against capital control. Before we do that, let us present some background material.

Capital Account Liberalization and Currency Crises

As mentioned above, in the Mundell-Fleming model for a small open economy with a fixed exchange rate and perfect capital mobility, the money supply that equilibrates the money market is given exogenously. This means that such an economy has no independent monetary policy. Any attempt by the central bank to raise the domestic interest rate above the world rate (plus a risk premium) will invite foreign capital inflow while any attempt to lower the domestic rate below the world rate will lead to capital outflow. On the other hand, if there is a change in the world interest rate, the domestic rate has to change accordingly. As a result, it is argued that there is inconsistency between the policy of simultaneous currency pegging and capital account liberalization for small open economies.

As a matter of fact, all the Asian and Latin American countries that experienced currency crises had various degree of capital account liberalization prior to the crises. A good example is Thailand. The passage of the Bangkok International Banking Facility in 1992 had resulted in a surge in foreign debts, a significant percentage of which went to the housing market. The eventual collapse of the housing market has contributed to the crisis in 1997.

In trying to apply the Mundell-Fleming model to explain the link between capital account liberalization and currency crises for these Asian and Latin American countries, three related points can be noted. First, for most countries, capital mobility is far from perfect: There are transactions costs, information asymmetry, heterogeneity between domestic and foreign assets, and administrative requirements. Because of the friction caused by these factors, domestic monetary policy cannot be effective, and domestic interest rates can deviate from foreign interest rates. Second, not all currency crises reflect inconsistent domestic policies. As the second-generation models emphasis, crises can be self-fulfilling. This seems to be what the ERM breakdown of 1992 suggests.

Self-fulfilling currency crises can be due solely to the actions of speculators, but the existence of domestic difficulties and huge external debts can also trigger self-fulfilling crises. In particular, when an economy is showing signs of difficulties, investors would want to move their capital out of the country and foreign lenders would refuse to provide more loans.

Third, most of these countries experienced not only a currency crisis but also a bank crisis. With the imperfection of and lack of sufficient supervision in the domestic banking system, the ability of domestic banks and financial institutions to borrow from -abroad makes the economy vulnerable. Both overborrowing (from abroad) and overlending (to domestic investors) could occur, and any widespread failure of some important sectors could trigger loss of investors' confidence, bank run, and financial crisis. On the other hand, if the problems of the domestic financial institutions are confined to the domestic economy so that foreign lenders regard these problems as short term, domestic financial institutions could raise new capital from abroad to help them solve the illiquidity problems.

A Historical Look at the Capital Account Liberalization

Exchange rate restrictions were unheard of in the period before World War I. Even during the war, pressures on exchange rate were easily avoided by official reserve holdings and credit operations. The stabilization of exchange rate was relatively easier as there were no historical memories of wars leading to severe realignments. The most memorable war was Franco-German war of 1870, which did not affect the currency of victorious nation, while leaving the currency of the defeated country depreciated by a mere 3½ %.

The failure to establish international monetary stability during the inter-war period led to trade restrictions and capital controls. The sentiments did not change even after World War II. Controls in the post World War II were generally targeted to achieve balance of payments objectives or as a part of broader economic development strategies (in addition, there were restrictions on current international transactions). The exchange controls in the UK were designed to protect sterling in the face of a weak balance of payments problem. The controls in the US in the 1960s were aimed at improving a weak balance of payments by preventing capital transfers abroad.

The controls in Japan and France ensured that savings were invested at home than abroad, while those in Germany and Switzerland were aimed at restricting capital inflows to prevent the exchange rate from appreciating. These restrictions were consistent with members' obligations under the IMF's Articles of Agreement. For example, Article IV, Section 3, states that "Members may exercise such controls as necessary to regulate international capital movement." The rationale was to prevent short-term equilibrating capital movements rather than long-term ones.

However, by 1958, the current account restrictions were removed in Western Europe and industrial countries waited until the end of 1970s to remove the capital controls.

The UK suspended all exchange controls in 1979, while Japan dismantled restrictions on capital movements in 1980, Australia and New Zealand in 1983, the Netherlands in 1985, France Sweden and Denmark in 1989, Norway, Belgium and Luxembourg in 1990, Finland and Austria in 1991, Portugal and Ireland in 1993 and Iceland in 1994.

Some of the developing nations have been liberal on capital account, like the Middle East oil exporting countries, Singapore, Hong Kong, Panama and Liberia. Indonesia opened its capital account in 1970, while Uruguay maintained a liberal capital account for a number of years.

CAPITAL ACCOUNT CONTROL: SOME CONVENTIONAL ARGUMENTS AND COUNTER-ARGUMENTS

Capital account control or liberalization is an old issue. Many arguments have been suggested to support capital account control, but many have also been made to argue for capital account liberalization.

We present some of the more traditional ones here. In the next sections, we will focus on those that are more relevant to the current Asian crisis.

Volatility of Short-Term Capital

Proponents of capital controls argue that controls help limit volatile short-term capital flows (avoiding balance of payments crises, exchange rate volatility, etc) and provide greater independence of interest rate policy. Financial markets are very liquid and react quickly to shocks, while the real economy is slow to react due to price and wage rigidities and investment irreversibility. Tobin (1978) and Dornbusch (1986) argue that this differential speed of adjustment, together with exogenous excess volatility in financial markets, may induce excess exchange rate volatility (over shooting, bubbles, etc) with negative effects on real economic activity. While Tobin proposes "throwing sand in the wheels" of short-run capital flows by imposing a uniform tax on all foreign exchange transactions, which would discourage very short-term capital flows, but with negligible effects on long run ones, Dornbusch suggests adoption of measures such as dual exchange rate systems, which would partially protect the real economy from fluctuations in the financial markets.

Opponents of capital controls argue that controls are particularly ineffective in preventing short-term movements, and the degree of insulation of monetary policy is therefore very limited. Large capital movements tend to occur when interest rates and exchange rates are out of line with fundamentals and therefore indicate the need for more timely adjustments in exchange rates and interest rates. Since it is difficult to distinguish between short-term and long-term investment and also between direct and portfolio investment, hence imposing controls on short-term inflows could crowd out the long-term foreign investment.

Protection of Foreign Reserves

Proponents of capital controls argue that controls support the balance of payments by protecting the foreign exchange reserves by preventing outflows of domestic savings and capital flight. Unstable macroeconomic and political environment in many developing economies can reduce the expected private returns from holding domestic financial instruments, and hence risk averse savers may prefer to hold a significant portion of their wealth in foreign assets that are perceived to yield higher or more certain real returns. Controls help retain domestic savings by reducing the return on foreign assets through interest equalization tax or by raising the costs of moving funds abroad) and by limiting access to foreign funds.

Opponents of capital controls argue that because of the scope for avoidance through trade and other channels, capital controls are ineffective in preventing outflows, but can discourage inflows and may not necessarily protect the balance of payments. In addition, even if capital controls limit the acquisition of foreign assets, they may still be ineffective in increasing and sustaining the availability of savings for domestic capital formation. If domestic financial instruments carry relatively uncertain and low real rates of return and residents cannot acquire foreign assets, they often respond by reducing their overall savings or by holding their savings in inflation hedges such as real estate or inventories.

Limitations on Foreign Ownership of Domestic Assets

Proponents of capital controls argue that controls limit foreign ownership of domestic factors of production. These controls prevent either unwarranted depletion of a country's natural resources or the emergence of a monopoly in a particular industry.

Equity and income distribution considerations are often cited as justifications for limiting ownership of domestic factors of production and real estate. Opponents of capital controls view controls as discouraging foreign direct investment. FDI may be an important source of external finance and the acquisition of new technologies.

Taxation of Domestic Financial Activities, Income and Wealth

Proponents of capital controls argue that controls are needed to maintain the authorities' ability to tax financial activities, income and wealth. Since domestic residents have an incentive to shift some portion of their financial activities and portfolio holdings abroad to avoid taxes on income from interest and dividends, controls are viewed as limiting holdings of foreign assets or to gaining information on the scale of residents' external asset holdings so that these holdings can be taxed.

Opponents of capital controls argue that governments can impose measures such as high reserve requirements that raise the demand for money and, hence, the inflation tax base. But this is detrimental in the long run as it raises rates of interest and hence discourage capital accumulation. Also, restricting foreign investment could slow market development, domestic investment and growth. Controls often breed bribery and rent seeking activities; this mentality could spill over to tax system and provide avenues for expansion of underground economies.

Insulation of Domestic Structural Reform Programs from Foreign Shocks

Proponents of capital controls argue that controls help in stabilization and structural reform programs. An early opening of capital account can cause a real appreciation, because of high interest rates typically associated with a stabilization plan and increased real exchange rate volatility. These would make trade liberalization more problematic. The credibility of the stabilization program plays a key role in determining the consequences of free capital mobility. For e.g., if a stabilization program lacks credibility, the liberalization of the capital account could lead to currency substitution and capital flight, which could trigger a balance of payments crisis, devaluation and inflation.

If the plan is credible, the high interest rates associated with a stabilization program may cause temporary large capital inflows. Sterilization of capital flows makes the interest rates remain high, encouraging further inflows and hence imposing a quasi-fiscal cost on the central bank. In the absence of sterilization, increase in money supply could jeopardize control of inflation. If nominal exchange rate is allowed to appreciate, it may deter trade reforms aiming at lower barriers to imports. Even if there was uncertainty about the likely success of the reform program, a capital inflow could occur if residents temporarily repatriate funds abroad to take advantage of the high real rates of interest. Opponents of capital controls feel that there are advantages in liberalizing the capital account simultaneously with domestic financial sector reforms.

Capital account liberalization will reinforce policies to liberalize domestic interest rates and the domestic economy more generally and to help create a competitive and efficient financial system. The increase in net private capital inflows, which tend to accompany the capital account liberalization, will help to support balance of payments during the period of domestic financial sector liberalization. In addition, capital controls reduce the credibility of government promises that international investors will be able to repatriate their funds. An open capital account, with a threat for capital outflows, and of short-term capital flows in either direction, could have a disciplining effect, making the authorities careful in their macroeconomic management.

Short-term Relief from Speculative Attacks

While proponents of capital controls argue that control program may help government buy time to move the fundamentals to a region where self-fulfilling speculative attacks are less likely, the opponents hold the view that the possibility that controls might be introduced in the future can generate attacks where none would be observed otherwise.

Lowering Local Interest Rates

Proponents of capital controls argue that controls help reduce the local interest rates without allowing capital outflows, so that investment could be encouraged. The opponents feel that capital controls are perceived as an additional risk factor by the investors. Hence, instead of reducing interest rates and limiting outflows, controls would require higher risk premia, and so would lead to higher interest rates to compensate for higher risk.

THE CURRENT DEBATE ON CAPITAL ACCOUNT LIBERALIZATION

Some argue that controls have played an important role in virtually all systems of pegged exchange rates since WW II. The controls give authorities some autonomy to preserve the peg, some space to organize orderly realignments and make it easier to ward off the speculative attacks. Others argue that capital controls were always easy to evade and never played an important role in limiting exchange rate flexibility. Dooley (1995) argues that controls have influenced yield differentials across countries, but there is no evidence that controls have helped governments achieve policy objectives, such as avoiding real appreciation, or that controls have enhanced welfare as the theory suggests. In addition, Johnston and Ryan (1994) and Grilli and Milesti-Ferretti (1995) find empirically that controls do not affect economic variables, like volume and composition of private flows, changes in foreign reserves or level of exchange rate.

In fact, controls are associated with higher inflation and lower real interest rates. Eichengreen et al (1996b) show that capital controls make a difference. Using data for 20 countries over the period 1962-92, they show that capital controls have been associated with significant differences in the behavior of macroeconomic variables such as budget deficits and money growth rates, but not in case of interest rates and foreign exchange reserves. However, Vinals (1996) argues that this is an evidence of controls being ineffective. In fact, Eichengreen, et al (1996b) find that periods when capital controls are effective are associated with inflation and high trade deficits.

This leads Vinals (1996) to argue that capital controls help authorities follow expansionary polices. Since such polices are associated with fundamental imbalances, capital controls eventually lead to exchange market turbulence and to unavoidable devaluations. Hence, controls make "self-fulfilling" attacks justified.

In short, Vinals (1996) believes that "capital controls do not seem to facilitate the defense of exchange rate stability in the short-run but continue to undermine it in the medium term through relaxation of policy discipline and coordination."

Reinhart and Smith (1997) argue that capital controls of the 1990s are asymmetric (they are imposed to discourage inflows) and are temporary. The temporariness is either pre-announced or the market rightly perceives them to be temporary as they are counter-cyclical. Even if they are intended to be permanent, they end up being temporary as investors find ways to circumvent the controls, making them ineffective.

They study the welfare consequences of taxes on capital inflows, and study the shock to the world interest rate that generates a surge in capital inflows. They find that if countries let the controls in effect for longer time period than the world interest rate is in effect, then it becomes costly because it causes the domestic real interest rate to rise once the temporary shock disappears, offsetting the benefits associated with smoothing the shock.

Stiglitz (1998) argues that increase in capital flows to developing countries increased the vulnerability of these economies to crises. He suggests some necessary, but not sufficient, conditions to deal with the capital flow problems.

First, there should be more information and greater disclosure, which would avoid triggering and exacerbation of crises. But the caveat is that markets don't fully incorporate all the information as the world is dominated by private-to-private capital flows.

Second, emerging markets could create more robust financial markets, more transparent systems of corporate governance, and less error-prone macroeconomic policy. But again, developing countries have less capacity for financial regulation and greater vulnerability to shocks.

Third, intervention in case of short term flows, which bring no ancillary benefits, besides trade credits, in an economy where saving rates are already high, but increase the vulnerability of an economy.

Krugman (1998c) also suggests that temporary capital controls could bring a respite for the suffering Asian countries. However, Friedman (1998) thinks that this is the worst possible choice, as the emerging countries need external capital (and the discipline and knowledge that comes with it) to make the best use of their capacities.

He suggests either a currency board arrangement or a floating exchange rate. Under the former, a balance of payments deficit automatically shows up in a decrease in high-powered money, and hence the discipline of external transactions is maintained, which is not possible under a pegged exchange rate system.

Under the latter, changes in exchange rate absorb the pressures that would otherwise lead to a crisis in a pegged exchange rate while maintaining domestic monetary independence. According to Friedman, the present crisis is not a result of market failure, but that of governments intervening in or seeking to supercede the market both internally via loans, subsidies or taxes and other handicaps, and externally via the IMF, the World Bank and other international agencies.

While Rodrik (1998) advocates capital controls because governments otherwise have to carry out policy based on "what 20 or 30-foreign exchange dealers in London, New York and Frankfurt" think, Henderson (1998) is of the opinion that "foreign exchange markets are a continuing, minute-by-minute election in which everyone with wealth at stake, including residents of the country, gets to vote, an election in which the winners are those countries whose governments have the most pro-growth policies". In his opinion, capital controls allow governments to hide the damage their policies do, which leads them to even-more-damaging policies.

Rodrik (1998) and Bhagwati (1998b) argue that free trade is not the same thing as free capital flows. Rodrik thinks that financial markets are different from goods and services markets in that the former are prone to market failures arising from asymmetric information, incompleteness of contingent markets and bounded rationality.

In fact, Bhagwati suggests that countries like India and China, which still haven't shed their controls on capital should not do that until they have attained political stability, sustained prosperity and substantial macroeconomic expertise. They should instead concentrate on internal reforms like privatization and external reforms like freer trade. They should allow targeted convertibility for dividends, profits and invested capital for direct foreign investment, as this brings in capital and skill and is more stable than short-term capital flows.

Unlike Stiglitz and Krugman, Bhagwati feels that the free capital economies, which are currently afflicted by panic-driven outflows, should not jump into capital controls. These countries need to restore the confidence. Capital controls, such as in Malaysia, can help lower interest rates to boost the economy, but if diffidence increases, who will borrow to invest?

Like Rodrik, Bhagwati (1998a) feels that the pro-capital free movement has dominated because of the self-interest of Wall Street financial firms, which see the free capital mobility world as an arena to make money. "Wall Street has an exceptional clout with Washington because of networking of like-minded luminaries among the powerful institutions-Wall Street (Altman went from Wall Street to Treasury and bank), the Treasury Department (Secretary Rubin is from Wall Street), the State Department, the IMF and the World Bank (James Wolfensohn, President of the World Bank, was as investment banker; Ernest Stern, managing director of J.P. Morgan, served as an acting president of the World Bank) most prominent among them".

SEQUENCING CAPITAL ACCOUNT LIBERALIZATION

It is widely accepted that capital account liberalization benefits economic growth: by improving the ability to tap savings globally at lower costs; enhancing the domestic agents' portfolio choices; improving resource allocation through increased competition for financial resources; and increasing the availability of resources to support investment, and to finance trade and other activities.

Michel Camdessus, Managing Director of the IMF, believes that "the trend towards capital account convertibility is "irreversible", and all countries have an important stake in seeing that the process takes place in an orderly way." Since the benefits from free capital markets are undeniable, then the costs and risks need to be minimized. Stanley Fisher, IMF First Deputy Managing Director, feels that there is a consensus that "liberalization without a necessary set of preconditions in place may be extremely risky." These preconditions are (IMF Survey 1998):

a sound macroeconomic policy framework; in particular, monetary and fiscal policies that are consistent with the choice of exchange rate regime;

a strong domestic financial system, including improved supervision and prudential regulations covering capital adequacy, lending standards, asset valuation, effective loan recovery mechanisms, transparency, disclosure, and accountability standards, and provisions ensuring that insolvent institutions are dealt with promptly;

a strong and autonomous central bank; and timely, accurate and comprehensive data disclosure, including information on central bank reserves and forward operations.

The optimal sequencing of capital account liberalization is complicated. Since all countries are different-in their levels of economic and financial development, in their existing institutional structures, in their legal systems and business practices, and in their capacity to manage the liberalization process-there is no single rule for sequence of steps to undertake in financial and capital account liberalization and no guideline for how the process should take.

There have been differing views, however, about the sequencing issue. While some believe that capital account should be liberalized following the liberalization of the current account and the domestic financial system, others hold the opinion that there should be simultaneous liberalization of the current and capital accounts.

Liberalization of direct investment is seen as a significant part of the real sector reforms, while liberalization of portfolio investment flows is coordinated with financial sector reforms and the development of financial markets and instruments. However, there are certain advantages in coordinating the liberalization in the financial sector and capital accounts:

The freedom of international capital flows reinforces the policies to liberalize domestic interest rates and helps create a competitive and efficient domestic financial system. The institutional reforms required could be mutually beneficial to both; e.g., creation of efficient money and foreign exchange markets.

Since capital account liberalization encourages the return of flight capital and eliminates impediments to inflows of foreign investment, it could support the balance of payments during periods of financial sector liberalization, when lifting of domestic credit controls initially leads to rapid increase in bank credit than deposits, increasing domestic resource pressures as banks run down holdings of excess liquidity, and weaken the balance of payments.

Many developing and transition economies already have a de facto high degree of currency convertibility, and openness of these economies means that even small changes in the invoicing or timing of exports and imports can result in movements of foreign exchange relative to GDP.

Maintaining controls under these circumstances results in pronounced balance of payments statistical discrepancies, which complicate the interpretation of underlying economic trends, and obscures the interrelationships between the domestic and external financial conditions.

Since the preconditions for capital account liberalization do not seem more onerous than those for domestic financial liberalization, hence the two should take place simultaneously.

The direct controls on interest rates and credits need to be replaced by indirect controls, as there is scope for avoidance of direct controls through capital movements. Hence, the adoption of indirect monetary controls should either precede or occur simultaneously with liberalization of capital account.

In fact, these reforms should take place early in domestic financial liberalization, as interest rates need to be market determined, and opening of capital account may have little impact on interest rate policy.

If the sequencing is not followed appropriately; then there are potential risks from opening the capital account. Continued reliance on credit controls or high non-interest bearing reserve requirements for monetary controls, and failure to address properly inefficiencies in domestic financial markets resulting in wide spreads between deposit and lending rates, may encourage borrowing abroad rather than domestically.

Inappropriate incentives for foreign borrowing may also be provided by the tax system, leading to an overvalued exchange rate and excessive external debt burden. Even if domestic financial and capital account liberalization do not proceed simultaneously, one should clearly recognize that there is a danger of removing most restrictions on capital account transactions before major problems have been addressed in domestic financial system. The problems include: inadequate accounting, auditing and disclosure practice.

Bibliography

Aliber, R. Z.: *The International Market for Foreign Exchange*, New York, Praeger, 1969.

Arestis, P.: *Money, Pricing, Distribution and Economic Integration*, London and New York, Macmillan and St. Martin's Press, 1997.

Ariel Buira: *Challenges to the World Bank and IMF: Developing Country Perspectives*, London, Anthem Press, 2003.

Arrow, Kenneth J.: *Social Choice and Individual Values*, New York, Wiley, 1951.

Ashok, Vasant: *Indian Economy in the World Setting*, Bombay, Himalaya, 1988.

Baldassarre, M. : *Building the New Europe*, London, MacMillan, 1993.

Bandow, Doug, and Ian Vasquez: *Perpetuating Poverty: The World Bank, the IMF, and the Developing World*, Washington, DC: Cato Institute, 1994.

Besley, T.: *How do Merket Failures Justify Interventions in Rural Credit Markets?*, Washington, D. C., World Bank, 1994

Bhagwati, J.: *Trade, Balance of Payments and Growth: Essays in Honor of C. P. Kindleberger*, Amsterdam, North-Holland Publishing Company, 1971.

Bhagwati, Jagdish: *India in Transition: Freeing the Economy*, Oxford, Clarendon Press, 1993.

Bhuleshkar, Vasant: *Indian Economy in the World Setting*, Bombay, Himalaya, 1988.

Cencini, A.: *Time and the Macroeconomic Analysis of Income*, London and New York, Pinter Publishers, 1984.

Chaudhuri, Pramit: *The Indian Economy: Poverty and Development*, New York, St. Martin's Press, 1979.

Connolly, M.: *The International Monetary System: Choices for the Future*, New York, Praeger, 1983.

Cooley, Thomas F.: *Frontiers of Business Cycle Research*, Princeton University Press, 1995.

Davidson, P.: *Money and the Real World*, London: Macmillan, 1978.

Desai, Vasant: *A Study of Rural Economics: A Systems Approach*, Bombay, Himalaya, 1983.

Dhingra, C.: *The Indian Economy: Resources, Planning, Development, and Problems*, Delhi, Sultan Chand, 1983.

Dornbush, R.: *International Economic Policy*, Baltimore, The Johns Hopkins University Press, 1979.

Downs, Anthony: *An Economic Theory of Democracy*, New York, Harper and Row, 1957.

Edwards, S.: *Capital Controls, Exchange Rate and Monetary Policy in the World Economy*, Cambridge, Cambridge University Press, 1995.

Gerald, K.: *The Less Developed Countries in the International Economy*, Cambridge, Cambridge University Press, 1975.

Greer, Douglas F.: *Industrial Organization and Public Policy*, MacMillan Publishing Company, 1992.

Guhan, S.: *The World Bank's Lending in South Asia*, Washington, Brookings Institution, 1995.

Hart, Oliver: *Firms, Contracts, and Financial Structure*, Clarendon Press, Oxford, 1995.

Hauft, Ottomar: *Distribution of Stock of Money*, Effingham, London, 1892.

Herin, J.: *Flexible Exchange Rates and Stabilization Policy*, Boulder, Westview Press, 1977.

Hinshaw, R,: *Monetary Reform and the Price of Gold*, Baltimore, The Johns Hopkins University Press, 1967.

Huang, Chi-fu: *Foundations of Financial Economics*, Prentice-Hall, 1988.

Jack Kemp: *A Monetary Agenda for the World Economy*, Boston, Quantum, 1984.

Jha, P.R.: *Agriculture and Economic Development*, New Delhi, Ashish, 1988.

Johnson, H.: *The Economics of Common Currencies*, London, George Allen & Unwin Ltd., 1973.

Kegan, K. : *Money and the Mechanism of Exchange*, MacMillan, London, 1890.

Kemp, J.: *A Monetary Agenda for the World Economy*, Boston, Quantum, 1984.

Lawrence H. White: *The Theory of Monetary Institutions*, Oxford, Blackwell, 1999.

Le Prestre, Philippe: *The World Bank and the Environmental Challenge*, London, Associated University Presses, 1989.

Magliveras, Konstantinos D. *Banks, Fraud and Crime*, Lloyd's of London Press, London, 2000.

McCallum, J. : *Global Disequilibrium*, London, MacMillan, 1992.

McLellan, Elisabeth P.: *The International Monetary Fund: Overview, Issues and Bibliography*, Happague, NY: Nova Publishers, 2002.

Michael Connolly, *The International Monetary System: Choices for the Future*, New York, Praeger, 1983.

Milton Friedman: *"Monetary Policy for the 1980s"*, Stanford, Hoover Institution Press, 1984.

Ottomar, H.: *Distribution of Stock of Money*, Effingham, London, 1892.

Paul, Kegan : *Money and the Mechanism of Exchange*, Oxford, London, 1890.

Peet, Richard, Born, Beate: *Unholy Trinity: The IMF, World Bank, and WTO*, New York, Zed Books, 2003.

Polak, J.J. : *The New International Monetary System*, New York, Columbia University Press, 1978.

Raj, K.N.: *New Economic Policy*, Delhi, Oxford University Press, 1986.

Ranade, Sudhanshu: *Rural Banking Adrift*, Bombay, Jaico Publishing House, 1984.

Rao, M.G. and R.J. Chelliah: *Survey of Research in Indian Fiscal Federalism*, National Institute of Public Finance and Policy, New Delhi, 1991.

Robert Z. Aliber: *The International Market for Foreign Exchange*, New York, Praeger, 1969.

Sebastian Edwards: *Capital Controls, Exchange Rate and Monetary Policy in the World Economy*, Cambridge, Cambridge University Press, 1995.

Seligman, E. R. A. : *Currency Inflation and Public Debts*, New York, 1922.

Sinha, R.K.: *Economic Development since Independence*, New Delhi, Deep and Deep, 1988.

Summner, Prof. : *History of American Currency*, MacMillan, New York, 1874.

Swoboda, A. : *Monetary Problems of the International Economy*, Chicago, University of Chicago Press, 1969.

Tremblay, R.: *Africa and Monetary Integration*, Montreal, Les Editions HRW, 1972.Adams, T.F.M. : *A Financial History of the New Japan*, Kodansha International Ltd., Lokyo, 1972.

Vines, David and Christopher Gilbert: *The IMF and its Critics: Reform of the Global Financial Architecture*, Cambridge, Cambridge University Press, 2004.

Wolfe, J.N.: *Value, Capital and Growth*, Chicago, Edinburgh University Press. 1968.

Index

□□□